A Child of Many Waters

Erin Lierl

Foreword by John Clark

Lavender Ink
New Orleans

A Child of Many Waters
Erin Lierl
Foreword by John Clark
Copyright © 2020 by Erin Lierl and Lavender Ink,
an imprint of Diálogos Books

Printed in the U.S.A.
First Printing
10 9 8 7 6 5 4 3 2 1   20 21 22 23 24 25

Cover and frontis art by the Author
Interior photographs by the Author
Book design: Bill Lavender

Library of Congress Control Number: 2020939171
Lierl, Erin
A Child of Many Waters / Erin Lierl
with John Clark (foreword)
p. cm.

ISBN: 978-1-944884-80-2 (pbk.)

Lavender Ink
New Orleans
lavenderink.org

Foreword

In Erin Lierl's beautiful and revelatory book, *A Child of Many Waters*, we are repeatedly thrown into the midst of things. Each moment is a wonder-filled, ironic, dialectical beginning that is a non-beginning.

Some will be struck by the sadness that pervades many of these moments. They take us into the world of *samsara*, the insubstantial world of constant change, of suffering and loss. This is the world of *sarvam dukham*, "all is sorrow." The book is faithful to the reality of this sadness.

But that is far from the end of the story. The work also announces the good news that the world of samsara is at the same time the world of nirvana, a world of joy, of the sacred, of deliverance. Every line in the text gives evidence, whether directly or more subtly, for Hakuin's statement that "This very ground on which we walk is the Pure Lotus Land."

Another core lesson from the book is that ours is also the world of *sarvam anityam*, "all is impermanence." All things are best seen not as things, but as flows momentarily converging into "things," "objects," "beings," and then separating again. The text repeatedly reminds us of this no-nature of things. "They are and aren't." "One world leads into another." "Things go on becoming."

In short, everything flows. There are almost a hundred references to rivers and streams in the text. Much of the work takes the form of a flow of personalities, thoughts, feelings, emotions, sensations, perceptions. Often, we learn only a little about the characters who appear, but we discover, at the same time, a richness and density of experience within the fleeting narrative spaces they inhabit.

Moreover, as we wade into this work's many waters, we step not only into a stream of consciousness, but also into a stream of coming-to-consciousness. This work is a stream of awakening. It helps us become aware, above all, of the nature and non-nature of the self.

A famous philosopher once asked what I would find if I "enter most intimately into what I call myself." The book gives us a much more compelling answer to this question than do most works of philosophy. At times, it presents an extraordinarily detailed phenomenology of selfhood, or non-selfhood.

> There's no one *in* here—just a racket, things knocking together. A void filled with incidental objects, a random assemblage of parts, making a clatter—space, sparsely ornamented with squiggles and dots.

But this is only part of the picture. There is a logic to all this racket, and the logic has a lot to do with the nature of our illusion of self.

> Who is making all this noise? The mental activity has a location. It is on the right side, in the back. There are other activities going on in other places. There is the place that says, "This is not good enough." A counterpoint, the voice that says, "I am ok, no matter what." This part of the mind has a water-faucet smile, buddha-smile. On the left side, in the back. A fear-voice, the voice of death, that finds a precipice of ruin in everything. This is a frontal voice.

This voice is one of the key characters in the book. One of the indispensible insights that Lierl shares along the way is that "The brain is tricky and a little stupid. It doesn't seem to want to be free." This is, we must understand, a book about liberation. Its dharma has one taste, the taste of freedom. But, as Lierl shows us vividly, we flee in fear from that freedom, haunted by that "frontal voice" in various forms, human and divine. We are intimidated by this voice that disciplines, constrains, inflicts guilt and suffering, and spawns delusion and mental confusion.

We are obsessed with defense of the ego, with worrying whether "others will notice" and judge us. In reality, she concludes, "There is only one witness, the one that has seen all. 'You who wove me in the womb.'" The book documents carefully the struggle with the life and death question of whether this witness will remain a kind of ultimate judge, the Big Other who will notice everything, or become a source of liberation from all judgment.

Yet, the book also reveals to us another voice, the poetic voice of creation, affirmation, and liberation. "Poetry is only form. Nothing, just form," says Erin Lierl. "Form is emptiness, emptiness form" says the *Heart Sutra*. Poesis is an exercise in a certain radical form of non-authorship, in not possessing the text. The author is no longer a Godlike figure, but rather like a God that is not God, an incarnational God, a God who knows how to die, and thus how to breathe life into the text. This is poetry as perpetual resurrection of the word.

Lierl askes the same question that Laozi asked at the beginning of civilized domination, when things began to fall apart. How can I become the ravine of the world, claiming nothing, but making everything possible? As she formulates it, "Can I get low enough to cast no shadow at all? Only then will I find life—when I expect nothing." This is the kind of negative capability, the doing-without-doing, the *wuwei*, that is the peculiar gift of the poet.

The many waters that are released by poesis are, in one sense, the many selves and non-selves that flow, momentarily, through the narrow channel that we misguidedly call "self." As Dogen famously stated, "To study the self is to forget the self, and to find realization in the Ten Thousand Things." But, as Lierl shows, it is excruciatingly difficult to forget the self. "'I am not nothing!' A voice in me cries. So, I still have to learn to be nothing." We fear this forgetting, as if it will lead us to lose everything, while, in reality, there is everything to gain.

Lierl's narrative abilities are evident throughout the work, but her skill as a storyteller is particularly evident in her account of a visit with her eighty-eight-year-old Uncle Ben. He is a revered monk, spiritual director, and teacher. They share a love for Thomas Merton. For Uncle Ben, it is Merton, the brilliant but wide-eyed and safely orthodox young convert of *The Seven Story Mountain*. For Erin, it is Merton, the mature peace and justice activist, interpreter of Daoism and Zen, and towering figure in the quest for interfaith dialogue and understanding. The understanding between Erin and Uncle Ben is not quite mutual, but their dialogue is beautiful, touching, and in many ways, a revelation.

The book also deserves recognition as travel literature.

It is one of those unusual travel books in which the traveler is neither a sightseer nor an explorer, but a "follower of the way." Much of the traveling takes place in New Orleans, but it also winds through Florida, Mississippi, Kentucky, Ohio, Puerto Rico, Guyana, England, France, Italy, Greece, and Portugal. Through all this travelling, India and Tibet are never far away.

Though all these many places are present, there is more than enough about New Orleans to make it one of the best works ever written about the city. It contains not the slightest hint of the Bigeasyism that infects so much of even the better writing about the city. Instead, it gives expression to the small, difficult, and sublime details of a city that still has a chaos within itself. It offers passageways into the microregions and psychoregions, ethnoregions and mythoregions, that make up that chaos.

But all this takes its place within a larger world of worlds. This is a work suffused with deep love and compassion for real people, for living communities, and for the sacred ground on which we walk, the Earth. It focuses intently, though often subtly, on the ultimate questions of meaning and valuing. It grapples on every page with the problem of overcoming delusion, and with the quest to be truly for, and very much with, this world.

—John Clark
New Orleans, Bayou La Terre, May 2020

A Child of Many Waters

The rain played cards with me all day
All she talked about was you.
I lost, like I always do.

1

The city slips by like a woman taking off her gloves. Banana trees wave in the blue-black night. Clapboard houses look like memories of themselves, like stage props, eaten by vines. Highways howl. Gas stations loom like alien craft, their lights blinding. Pot-bellied men move slowly in parking lots. The safety of citizenship crumbles like a clod of earth, runs down the sides of the sinking metropolis, skates into an abyss with breath of blood.

A ramp lifts us from the dregs of streets, dizzy in their terrifying stasis. We float through an icy wind of billboards, over an expanse of orange glowing globes. Refinery chimneys draped in yellow light oversee their domain like smug grandfathers. All around, concrete hangs rippling in stages of unearthly suspension.

"Don't get lost," Sandiman says. "Be here."

"The world looks really scary," I say with effort.

"This is the world we grew up in. This is what we're from. We made it this way." He corrects himself: "The people before us made it this way."

"Why?"

"They didn't know how else to do it. How do you want them to divide, when all they know is how to add?"

A pink chemical smell wraps around the car and curls up in my nostrils. A factory roars alongside the highway. Nearer to the road a neon sign: "Nails."

I wrap the blanket over my head and grip the jar of hot water between my knees. Ahead, a wall of pink fog lies across the road like a curtain. Driving through it, we cannot see the lines of the road. I hold my breath. We emerge into empty road. Another curtain of fog lies ahead.

"This is scary," Sandiman says.

We pass the state line. The four 'S's of Mississippi hook together in extravagant loops. The road dips below the fog that hangs above like a ceiling. We don't speak. My eyes swim into my dark brain. Factories and refineries seep fluorescent smells. Sandiman pulls into a gas station and puts up the hood, then drives on.

"Are you warmer now?"

"Much better."

I hate the sound of my voice, dripping, oozing out of me.

Stars show through tears in the clouds. I don't want to look at the stars or go near the water.

"Just wait right there," Sandiman says. "I'll put the tent together."

He does it blindly, feeling with his hands in the dark.

I slide my feet through the icy grass.

When the sun is already high, we walk together to the water's edge. Sandiman smiles and yawns into his hands. I claw at myself from the inside. White birds run in the surf, poking their beaks into the sand.

"They're desperate," Sandiman says, amused.

The shells in the tide are stained orange. Clods of oil sit in the sand like smooth black rocks. Sandiman destroys sand-flea villages with his big toe.

"I want to sleep more," he says.

Pieces of jellyfish lie like marbles in the shallow water. I see a jellyfish, intact. He stabs it on a stick.

"These guys don't have any brains. They're just plasma." Sandiman repeats this, holding the dripping jellyfish aloft on the stick. He lowers it onto the sand.

"It's still alive!" I cry.

Slowly, the jellyfish contracts into a ball.

"I just killed it," Sandiman realizes out loud.

We watch the jellyfish harden, pulsing in the place where it has been pierced.

"Do you think you should put it back in the water?"

"It was dead there when we found it. It was just lying there."

"Put it back in the water."

"Do you want me to stab it again?"

I look away as he pokes the stick once more through the jellyfish and plops it back into the shallow water.

"It's dead. That's how we found it," he says.

Wind chimes prowl, roam in packs. Place has given way. I wake up poisoned. I do things automatically. This pull between my ribs—the ribs of an alien being. Thoughts make waves in my mind. Flesh hangs from bones. "Writing" opens its belly-drawers, full of nightmares and wisps of debris.

"You're creating this yourself," Sandiman would say. "You're making things bad."

But there is no sweetness here, no laughter—only defeated people with their bar tabs. Winter stretches out bleakly.

Wind chimes knock together. Stages sag under heavy fruits. Will I work again in the temple of forgetfulness?

Birds are singing. I have forgotten my mind. Forgotten my mind, I have forgotten my mind.

The Quarter is far away. Sandiman wanders in it. He unscrewed the bars of my window and hopped in.

"You can't do anything," he noticed.

For a long time, I have haunted.

"I love myself," Oreana's mother says, "when I read what I wrote in my journal in my twenties. I was going to start an orphanage, create a community. I didn't do any of it, but that's ok, because I did other great things. I wanted to be an accumulator of experience."

But beware any kind of accumulation.

Sandiman: "We were in the car a minute ago. Now we're under the tree. That moment is gone. It's dead."

Lucita says the past never dies.

They are both right.

Bikes rattle by. New Orleans, infected with development. I want to go up high, but there is no up-high. There is only the river—the river of death and the tree of life.

What can I find, what can I find. The end of things, the beginning of things. The moaning of the wind-chimes. The guts of civilization—find them everywhere.

What did I learn on the roadside? The hollowness of words—India with indecipherable eyes, India with ancient hunger. She looked past me, as if I weren't there.

This is me, vibrating like a bell. This is me, rippling like water. A woman who is no longer young, watching the lines fold on her face. Windows open and close their throats.

Hypnotic, uncleaned. I am at home with the wind-chimes and the space-heaters.

Perhaps there is only one story: the moan of the train, drained of all romance. The wheeze of the space-heater, laden with regret. This body, hung from these bones. Clapboard and hopes. The wind tears through our hairs.

"What if money had an expiration date?"

I woke from a deep sleep, before the alarm. Lucita sat up. Fatefully I started coffee. I put on work-pants, looked at myself in the mirror. We are all prisoners.

"For what is a nation-state but a prison with a flag on it?"

I will go out into the streets full of fog and uncoil my long yarn. The story of what? Of the city that disappeared. Police cars with their whines, their complaints. Cypresses drip orange-brown needles. Hear the train: mountainous sound, gorgeous gift of sound. Like a moaning beast, memory and the sea. Leaves quiver in the white sky. Wind chimes give their warning.

Sandiman bleeds out, becomes a myth, two-dimensional. I forget the exact face of his face. The end, in the hair of the willows. The truth in little rivulets.

The drunk boy asked me to dance three times, three times I said no. A man rubbed his crotch and stared at me. A lady with a pet rat told me her woes, her voice barely audible over the crowd. She wets herself. She is in the fourth stage of cancer. Her sons impregnate women without knowing their hearts—she beats her own breast: thunk, thunk. Everyone pointed their phones at one other. The musicians filmed the lady with the rat. She was drinking a long can of beer. Dirty young people on the curb smoked Pall Malls. Berenice played Professor Longhair.

Passing, women who want to die, women who want to live. The softly-slipping tongues of commerce, quietly destroying our lives. Patience barely filters down—we catch at it like money. A rain of anguish, a wet wind of anguish. A hot tongue of anguish, a broken bell of anguish.

A dream of being stalked by a bounty-killer and sleeping in a different house each night. In a cavern there were Native Americans with masks, with horns, floating on the shores of a river. I've dreamt them before, under dark trees, in water.

The waves lap upon the steps. They break and ripple, then become smooth. A plastic net holds the earth in place. Puddles in the muddy matted grass tremble in the wind. A pelican floats, turning in circles, then lands on the levee. A Doritos bag somersaults down the steps. A seagull walks through a puddle. The sun brightens and touches my skin. The lake turns green.

There is still some meaning to grasp. Our wants are ciphers in a forgotten language. We see them for their meaning, their implication. But they are no more than their form, a random shape. We are what has been forgotten.

Patrick passes by, healthier than before. A waltz ends. A homeless man is rousted from his slumber on the sidewalk. The weather is warmer. Something has changed. The mask-shop man leans, smoking, his legs crossed. Pineapple lights dance. Harmonicas throb. A red-eyed man lifts boxes into the new trash truck. He smiles at me—a flash of golden teeth—and waves a gloved hand. I remember: I was happy once.

Conditioned since beginningless time, rain has come. The twilight brightens as the streets begin to shine. The clouds are sails. Pink hangs behind the blue in a clot. The steel guitar player from Tennessee straightens his tie. My eyes blister with tears of unknown origin. The strings have clogged noses. They sing about mountains and redheads by the road, of umbrellas and memories that become shapeless, hiding under time. Beginningless time.

The sky has gone lavender—the most confusing place between blue and purple. Last night's fog made the world larger, artful in the branches of the trees.

Zorba: Your leash is longer than the leashes of most men. But the mind is like a grocer. It always keeps the leash intact. It takes folly to snap the leash.

A man dressed as a tree eats his food off the newspaper box. Another man leans on the Rouse's building with a sign: "Homeless. Thanks."

I hurried to finish the story—but it was written in me already. They all are. There are no more questions. I know in a place beyond words.

Berenice plays "Hot time in the Old Town Tonight." I can see time passing through her family's faces. Her husband plays the sousaphone and her young daughter plays the drums. A cloud passes over things. Raven, the fortune-teller, kisses me lewdly. Rain is coming. I seek things—as if I would find them in the streets, by looking.

Two young train-hoppers perform a gentle, dumb-eyed romance.

"I looked everywhere for a single person I could relate to, but I drank all my booze alone, and I still can't forget."

His eyes are streaked. He wears dreadlocks, orange overalls.

Berenice's music comes in and out like the tide.

"I'm not like Zorba," says my mind.

The warmth brings back memories: watching the glittering balconies, my cells purring, with Patrick in the twilight years ago.

A musician looks for a parking spot. The evening slips into its place. I wade through myself. The fog, with death in it. Rain. Blue in that piece of sky. A sadness that has no shape.

Walking across the train tracks, the sounds of trains, of boats, of insects, converged and ticked and sounded as I hoped they would. I was full of people. There are no words for these things. I can say "longing," but it is not enough. I miss people I don't know. Death closes in on the innocent things and the good things.

The pain is not real pain; it is the illusion of pain. Grey, thick and slow. The world doesn't look like me. I can't find myself in it. Reality is full of stories, things opening like flowers, like seeds opening. Little orgasms at the edges of things. Chills down my legs, wind chimes knocking together.

When was the last time I was in my skin? When did I begin believing in time? The wall grows darker: a winter evening wanes at my back. I hear the purring of cars over the wet street, the hissing of air pushing leaves over one another, the squeaking of a gate, and wind chimes. My eyes hunger for light. Pangs, sudden anguish. There is always a withholding, there is always an elaboration, there is always a bit of truth sliding down the cracks.

We will be safe from ourselves someday. Chaos fires in little chains. Memories crackle in my brain. I love everything. I wake up homeless and cool. A flock of long-necked birds reflecting in puddles. Strange weights lying on my spirit. What can be done? I am standing on nothing, floating in space. I grasp at filaments. I am falling, bumping against other falling objects. January hisses outside.

Frozen fingers hauling home the typewriter, thinking. Amar played the Santur: the delicate hammers, the gas fire dancing. Oreana, the sunlight creeping away. Berenice with her head back, singing. Wisdom has receded, curling down around my feet.

An emptiness is before me. An ocean of time, the slow melting of me into nothing. Raven clean-shaven kissing my hair. Sandiman's man's smell, his jacket cold after being outside. His room full of sky and rocks.

The cold in my fingertips, the hum of my mind. The mind, storing memories, making decisions. The illusion of continuity, of self. The brain is tricky and a little stupid. It doesn't seem to want to be free.

My heart stirs like a lady sleeping. The trees are like sterile old men. The dreams in us are proof—of what, I can't remember. Perhaps there is only the January sunlight and toothless old-man trees—the yard laden with Mardi Gras beads and Christmas lights and shadows that soften and harden, airplanes purring through the sky. In the mirror my face grows hollow. I miss people I don't know.

Sitting by the lake, I knew. I sketched the river-bend at dusk. My dreams are close to me, bubbling up, riding alongside me. Sonya with her doe-eyes, talking of escaping. Am I she? Or is she I? Bank envelopes, Virgin Mary candles, a hanging dress in the window. I am hurt by my leaving, and that is as it should be.

It's easy for people who have moved to the center to talk of pain that bears lessons. They should not forget about the people who live on the edge, where nothing is real, where pain is just pain—meaningless, futile pain.

I saw Patrick in the sun, taking air into himself, preparing to expel it in song. His features were hazed, but I could see his two grey alien eyes looking into mine. He smiled with song in his mouth.

I looked at the river and saw a real river. Walking along the bayou: white birds, fishermen, shells, the glint keeping up with me, grass bifurcating, sprawling up out of the cement.

Ladies sit in a row on the curb, their hair clipped and dyed like eunuchs, in sunglasses and newly-manufactured "tops." Edna is with me, getting tired in the water. Mardi Gras for a moment abates. The drunken fly in my red wine. Patrick's cowboy shirt with the design down the back—the peacock manner of the cowboy singers.

The street repeats scenes of other days. I see the shreds of things that have ended, the beginnings of things to come. Masks leer from balconies as the sun goes down. I remember that it is January—time of darkness, of shrill intoxication. The death that is in Mardi Gras, the swarming abyss of the beyond—then we wake up to Spring, having survived.

Something mysterious lies down at sunset. People walk away with their instruments cased. I lean after them, searching for a face—but whose?

A river runs under the days, under my mind. I pluck at my strings, but no one can hear me. I dreamed again of that city with its petals fallen, that purple-skied city after everyone has gone.

Full moon night. Parades in the neighborhood, spring warmth. Cypresses like arteries shooting up out of the sidewalks. Palms wave their blades on the twisting streets of the Marigny where for a moment I am alive. My body feels coarse and sore to the touch. I miss people being people. The people in the streets are not people but a crowd, weighted by what they're suffering through.

The lake water is dark. I woke with a wordless question—

I go back into myself. The week is lodged in eternity. The days take off their hats. Lamps burn, the temperature changes. Leaves wag and cars scar across the city, pass through it like a knife. Pierced by this movement, we change together.

I lay down my swords. They turn to groggy women, rub their eyes, lie on the pavement like worms, become shining puddles that reflect a sky full of power-lines. Music has left me. Words don't penetrate. The moon sometimes hides behind itself. Is that possible?

I wander through emptiness, a city where I feel like a ghost. It doesn't hurt. It's what's coming that hurts.

I put all my poems and notes in a paper bag and burn them beside the canal. Each of us knows the truth, as we know the moon is there even when it's hidden. Each of us knows, though our knowing be eclipsed. The stories are all in me.

The floors are strewn with glitter, feathers. My old friends look at me out of wells. Their faces waver greyly, their eyes are hopeful and not-hopeful at the same time. They want but know better than to expect. They plead but know the answer is not coming. They are and aren't. One world leads into another.

Wisdom, come down. There is a young man with a golden heart that goes on its way to be ruined by this country and its foul stinking patterns. Patterns of thought and patterns of pain. The train complains. Things go on becoming. I have broken the evening like a twig over my knee. Where are my stories?

Amar in the wind with living eyes. Pictures of flying birds in a glass cabinet. Fog on the river. St. Louis Cathedral lit with pink spotlights, news crews set up on the railroad tracks. Black heavy undulations shining.

Saturday with its lamps on, with its shoes off, the sky rumbling. The pain is a show, a reproduction of pain. There is chaos in me, and there are good things. The streets gurgle.

"I'm not ready!" someone cries.

Musicians are out, some with nice eyes and some with mean eyes. A brass band peppers the night. Horns discordant from three directions. Bounce music blasting from a passing truck.

A sudden whiff of freedom: night people strolling, somewhere a tambourine. A couple passes me, the man with a cane clinking. Voices in the steps of Cafe Rose Nicaud. Another year sings for its supper.

I can see the singer's bare back moving catlike, slowly, rocking back and forth before the microphone. She lifts her chin and her voice rolls out like red velvet. Dizzy brass sounds from DBA: the sounds of years past. A tuba and cymbal and a drum: the sound of Mardi Gras and forgetting.

Above the river there were the same stars as always. A rock was nearly covered by the opaque waters, full of death and unimaginable filth. Close to the mystery, I watch it where I'm perched. It's a gift to sit close to the mystery.

"It was a lovely and difficult time."

The strings of three guitars, moon-curves in the cheeks of brave young men—one like a mermaid on the bow of a ship, one like the moss that grows on a stone, and one like a steel rail, smelling of burning and reflecting the sky. The eyes of musicians—how they turn inward, how they meet one another and speak—their secret laughter—the elation that comes only after its source has passed.

Memories open like jewelry boxes with pop-up spinning

ballerinas—the sounds of roosters in the soft morning light, a tapestry undulating over a window, wind chimes in a tree, beads and stones, the smell of wire. I watch these ballerinas spin in circles. It is complete. And I am completion, with nothing to prove, nothing to expect from any man or woman.

Dryness in the garden. Nothing growing inside. All the old people are somewhere else. All the new people are somewhere else. I have put down some tools and not picked up others. I'm in the empty square, before square one. I watch my wanting swell, then go away. I have gone deeply into something, under something. I am somewhere without words, without cheeks or eyebrows, without clothes or pencils. I contract into a single point, an impossible entity—without size, without contour. It is malice. It is malice with no outlet, an implosion.

Crickets, laughter, engines. The city is seized by festival like a fever spasm. Its face is sinister. The revelers are large and brutish, their eyes strange, their attention fleeting. They wear shining plastic and colored wigs, and some of them smile like children.

The pain is like a dream, or a photograph of pain.

"You argue in your sleep," Sonya says.

A wet sludge on Frenchmen Street. Glittering people drift by like riverboats.

Even if he came, the noise would not stop. Night has fallen. Insects are singing. It is warm.

Heaviness is the root of lightness. The writing will fall off like a deformed fruit. I will go somewhere. I am afraid of it.

Musicians in Rosa's playing cards, playing piano, talking about getting out of town. The sky has a frightening cold in it and the bare branches scrape at the swirl of pale light. I will use what I can. The sky is diffused with melon pink. I rise too.

White pelicans float down the canal. When a fish jumps, the pelican paddles toward it. A fish jumps somewhere else, and the pelican follows it.

A chance rises out of me, like a soul leaving its body, steam-like, a scythe skating across the river. I am pushing leaves around with my toes in a whirlpool round a gutter.

I know with tremendous knowing about dark corners and pathetic truths. I avoid coarse edges. My heart is broken not for myself but for the others, for Amar and the streets we stand on, for the hurt that rips through the flesh of people, through their dignity, through the pieces of sidewalk, through the young and old.

I have been wanting the wrong way. My wanting has been a weapon, a vent for old resentments. I wanted as a substitute for the huge and nameless terror of being myself. All those passageways, all that fear.

Sandiman: an island cut adrift in the flow of the economy, doing his own photosynthesis, smiling on the flood of moments. Perhaps he is not there at all—only this stone lodged in the current, and I come to crash upon his apartness, his foreignness, finding there richness, like wind and sun together in a tree.

Those days sink under the horizon of December. These new days are raw, pull apart the curtains, show the abyss gaping all around.

In the rain by the river, I run clear of entanglements. May-flies are dying in the houses and schools. The river is not deep. Not deep with the depth of the work to be done. I touched the lamppost blistering with age and stood under the wreathed sky. I am the only one who has made this exact prison of her fantasy. No other touches this lamppost under this sky, in a prison just like this which I have delicately carved out of sea. I am not Edna, nor am I a chambermaid or chestnut seller, nor a dark-eyed death-cry streaking through her hatred, with her fingers against the jaws of a dead city. I am only my mother's daughter: a good woman no one wants.

I can scarcely hold the pen. The light refracts on my eyes. I hold myself carefully together, like a wire dancer. I've lost my keys, but they will find me—my steel keys like train-tracks smelling of loss. Wherever this city is climbing, I don't want to go.

Time flows over a cliff. Its long fingers lift dust and pebbles like a tongue. I don't bring anything out, just put things in. Growing big and swollen. Others leave the womb, but I stay inside, not ready. Time is canceling everything. Soon, there will be no more inside.

Reality fills up with time, now taking over the cliff, so there isn't any cliff, just the sea. I am not in touch with the deep of death, where my corpse will find me, where I will part ways with the face I have fought.

New Orleans keeps me in her lap, then gets bored and stands up. The cold gets inside me. Time goes on whipping. There is nothing to write. A skeleton in the sunset, the older people inside the young people—I see them coming out.

I wake with sadness for things happening far away. The weather is wet. It thunders. There is no feeling of time. What am I guilty of? Rain-drops tick. I think about my plan. I lay it to rest. I am tied to it through the belly.

Wind chimes tell stories in their language. The neighborhood clunks and purrs with weekend. A radio talks through a wall, someone throws things from a height. There is a murmur now and then as of someone sleeping.

I sang my ranchera and we listened to the rain. I felt my love for Sandiman die—a feeling in my heart like an eyelid going down. The world becomes real while I watch. There was always a world—a bike strung with beads, a black chair, an easel. Now I get back into my body, like someone coming through the window. I become real, the space and objects around me crystallize. They exist with me. We are real together.

Louisiana yesterday looked so much like herself, minty young green in the oaks and in the cypresses and in the palms. Caverns in me, sleeping fears, the birds wild in the trees, a dead love I drag around. I will take it apart and put it in the river.

Time wanders on, childlike, playing games. I hear Olive. A deep and soft love in me, a mint-green light.

Days that barb and sift and leave everything unopened,

repeat themselves. I listen for something that lives over the highway, over the CBD, something magenta and connected to the old days. The fortress of the present decomposes, disintegrates. I search and find nothing. The inner world is barren, jammed. I have lost my balance.

Moonlight behind clouds. My heart is sweet, giving off sweetness. I come out to meet the street like an expectant lover, stomach jumping. The disc of the moon is swept clean by clouds. After days without a glimpse of sky, it is a miracle to see. Tonight my angel returns to port. The moon is free! A whole swath of sky is cleared, is blue. A woman passes. Her face is good.

The temperature drops. Something reptilian sneaks into the moment. I am all knuckles, my kindness out of tune, the sky naked, my self down around my ankles. Open, open.

My naked writing: half-made, lame, awkward, twisted inward. My whole being is this way—not quite put-together, inverted and inept, ingrown, shadowy, redundant.

Now the whole sky is washed clear, and in my heart a sadness sits like a sleeping bird—it sleeps with its eyes open. Or is it simply the despair that comes with being—a by-product of non-being as it is being shed? Old rancors rise. Booze evaporates under the moon. Fierce hope drags misery behind it like a twist of vine.

The year rolls around in its bed—the black shoulders of the drummer shine in the window of the Spotted Cat. Puddles shake. I have been here all year, participating in its sleep, roaming around the edges of its glory, eyes turned always on an inner question.

I sat in the glowing front room of Lucita's house with a young man whose tuning pegs were broken. The silent deep trails leading to our selves were heavy. The only answer to such weight is eclipse, aversion, closing, waiting.

My throat catches as I think about what might have been—it overwhelms; how big things are, how gentle. Most of the story can't be seen. It happened in a shadow-realm beyond time, memory, accounting—it is lost. It was a fight in the dark with adversaries who have vanished, who may have only existed as props, hypothetically.

Magicians ruffle scarves. The crowd dissipates. The world rumbles. Time closes in, but lets me rest inside it, eternal. One glove on, the pen in my right hand, leaning on my typewriter table, filling with words this page like a well with fish swimming in it, some nearer and others further from the surface.

Sidles in an amazing discomfort with dimension itself. People walking seem to be upside-down, their faces turned backwards, their features rearranged—eyes where their mouths should be. They crowd together, talking out of their foreheads.

They walk without walking, carrying images of themselves in other places, with other faces. Each one murders the moment with a frightening will. They walk toward death with glum expressions, in boots, with shopping bags, the blood just a gesture of blood in their veins. They drag behind them parachutes filled with terrors, long dark hallways in their eyes. Their feet massage the street. Their shadows move under them like souls between worlds. They decay from the inside out.

There is a sound under everything. I am whole, but flimsy flags mark the longing, as if I were a landscape that nowhere, failing to be itself, assumed.

Failures fall like fruit from trees. Looking through me-holes, a tunnel of me wraps around the emptiness, and plumes of me-sadness stroke the emptiness, and me gets in the way of seeing the truth. I plan, hook myself to contingencies. I hope, I don't remember that I am already finished.

The world spreads its feathers, parades. I use my grocer's scales to think. Shadows claw, the reproaches of people once known but now only extrapolated.

Freed of my old self, I feel like a baby moose, wobbly in my knees, not sure what so much of me can do. Bells that don't ring are pinned to the window-frame. I hear bells that ring.

Walking over a plain of myself, a river of me lies under my path, while my small self scrambles on the surface, hauling things: a broken guitar, a net full of receipts, monkey-skulls, nicked marbles, rocks with eyes. Sandiman haunts my peripheries.

The trees look like what they are. Death is everywhere, grotesque and commonplace. The days pass like a silent parade, nothing happening.

Watching two men cross Orleans Avenue, each with his own way of knowing, being able, the concerns he addresses and the satisfaction with which he addresses them.

The paint on the sidewalks speaks to me. I walk with real being. Everything whines under the weight of "me," this monstrosity, this broken record, her invisible chains.

Can I face the people; shouldn't I hide? The train yard, the wharf, the river-walk, the bridge, the roofs slanting, the sun through an old window. I see myself in the city and curled up underneath it.

The sky has thought of everything. One mind has already swallowed everything. Nothing matters to that mind. It has always been ready, isn't interested in the birdcage.

Another mind can't stop looking under stones, opening doors where it will find things that hurt. It likes to cry, holding a shard of broken mirror in its hand.

Raven ushers me into my chair, jostling it open, kissing me, strutting off in his trench-coat, his knees turned out. A fiddle pulses. A magician heads home for the night. My face is old and parched. Children in strollers like severed heads. Girls in dresses and boots—blue-eyed girls with violins, banjos, sweet, clear yodels. People I knew wheel by, old now, delivering food. This little box contains terror.

"There's nothing wrong with you," I tell myself. "You are exactly what you are."

The river was intricate with ripples. The lights spilled down off the ferry: is it a dream? Red, white, yellow, streaking down the black river. A voice on a speaker—I couldn't understand the words. The paddle left a broad wake, and beyond it the river rose to the horizon like a wall.

I squatted, staring, for once merely obeying, free of will, watching the sun run down to the shore. A boat went by:

Crystal Island. I looked at the windows, the angle of the lines. There was a lot of world to look at. The buildings on the West Bank were lit golden. My suffering had its shoes off, waiting gently on the road.

I am tangled in myself. The world swirls around pain, the curve of space whereon ride tourists with high white socks and bulky camera cases, balding men with backpacks, pedicabs, taxi drivers like sculptures of stone, people from other states with colored drinks in plastic cups. Women melted and swollen by time, Americans like monkeys with shopping bags. Everyone looks sallow and deathly ill. I'm done, ring the bells. I'm done.

I am in love with love—I have more than I had before. Beside the river I knelt, and a pain was in me unlike other pains. The pain had grown to match my growth—it threatened to blow me over.

"This is you," I explained to myself. "This is the other side of joy."

A continent of pain, an ocean of it breaking and breaking and breaking. Opening, moving from inside to out, eating me steadily away—perhaps carving me into a shape that later I will recognize.

I get on. The ride sweeps under me. The ride turns to ash. I am dreaming. The beautiful, beautiful clouds of smoke they blow. My love is a dimple in space-time, and big people roll around it, and red-eyed perfect people roll around it, and staccato stylish people swing around it, and Americans roll around it.

A basic sadness, my illness gently unfolding—this sea of walls that love me, these old hands, a rising in my heart. Desolate people. The evening has a mystic face, a rock face.

I'm walking through a wet, foggy landscape, picking knots out of my hair, shaking my head. I'm looking for the good thing I left here. I know I left it here, but nothing can be seen. I go over my own tracks.

The trombonist is a virtuoso. The streets have in them the shadows of terror, the terrible mundane, the ceasing of struggles in the static emulsion of eternity.

See how we are prisoners—the money we earn, just to pay for the things we need, just to pay it back. We imagine freedom, but our bondage is renewed. The immaculate depression of the restaurant servers, their suspicious emphasis on their sanity. I feel I am underneath something, trapped.

Patrick looked beautiful, waving in the sun—good, like blood, like home. I am lost—everything vague, abortive, leading nowhere. The incredible brown eyes, wet in the evening light, of the mask shop man. A precise, kind harmonica down the block. A great loss lying over things, like a dusting of snow that reflecting the sky makes things brighter.

The sidewalks were lavender and blue, broken in the patterns of veins, speckled with oblong oak leaves in the sunshine.

I spoke with Raven: "What time do you get here?"

"I sleep in the street, darling."

I walked on, finding nothing I didn't already know.

Amar comes crossing the street and sits before me with his eyes from an ancient world.

The center of me is tied to my death like an umbilical cord. It will not be surprised. Its job is to pull me there.

Is every work of art an atonement for a breach with reality?

Along the city my eyes drag. Other people cannot know, cannot know what I know. What then matters? There's no one in here—just a racket, things knocking together. A void filled with incidental objects, a random assemblage of parts, making a clatter—space, sparsely ornamented with squiggles and dots.

Listless sun-soaked jug band in the miracle sun. Loss, in her blue jeans, with her gym-sculpted legs. The wrong man does the wrong dance and pulls a bottle of Evan Williams from his hip pocket. A woman claps hopelessly at her strollered infant. The hurt bursts and slides down like ink through heavy water. Nothing in me works. Everything is slow, sleeping.

Patrick speaks to me, more tattooed, more brittle than before, a stranger. When he sings, it's familiar. Even though I knew him briefly, long ago, I miss him.

"I'm leaving town in a week or so, myself."

He will bike to California. What then should I be afraid of? Everything is possible.

Girls take over the spot, singing bluegrass songs with banjo, fiddle, guitar, sundresses, flowers.

Helicopter seeds lie one-winged on the porch steps,

fading. The river is no longer a river—after seeing something so many times, it disappears. I work with my writing until there is nothing left—no story, no feeling, no message.

Being, peaceful, or being, dull. Being, mournful, being burning: a light that will extinguish. When was the first time you learned the sun would die? That everything disappears, betrays itself?

Hopelessness is also hope.

I move easily in a quiet, open city. This space is provided by violence. Where do words meet violence? Paper covers rock? No. Words don't solve matters of the heart. We can hold onto them only so far—then we leave them, bobbing, shimmering above.

Deeper still is the place where freedom and violence are made. Here, words have never been invented.

I woke, a handful of petals—the oracle herself in the wake of the whiskey.

What eyes look back at me out of the mirror?

"Is this a human being? What does it mean?"

My mind curls up like a snake. The city sighs.

Lidded, my eyes drift under sunlight. Sandiman ambles by. Our hands dance like birds: "It's ok now. It's ok."

I rise above the surface. Where have I been? I stride with long strides—I cover ground.

My typewriter is sealed in a chest beneath Victor's sacred objects. The musicians smoke, every one of them in the sunshine. The field that was burnt grows again. It sends up sweet purple shoots.

At the breakfast table, Victor spoke of hanging himself.

"Not happy, Aurora. Not happy."

He was old and glorious in his pajamas. My leaving makes him remember his age. His house sinks him into the earth. He takes the long way through his stories. I must wait for an answer, until I forget what I've asked.

In his sunhat in the car shop, he spoke to the mechanics. "Tengo primos en San Luis…"

He waved as I drove away. For a moment, he was smiling.

I don't look at people. I look at a light within. Nights of wandering, I see my city. The people are strewn, misplaced—beside the Carousel bar, the trombonist drunkenly opens his case and begins to play.

Sunlight on my sickness. Possibilities in the sounds of a string band. I hear things waiting—things I cannot know. A young man finger-picks, cigarette hanging from his mouth, boot tapping. His heart is there in my heart. He raps at the door of eternity. He tries to break in.

New Orleans goes about its business, takes no notice of us. Children dissolve, left too long soaking. Wishes run swimming among me. Women and men look on me. Children and old people look on me. The shade is cool and hard. My way is crinkled like an old pot. The great parade is yawning. The winter is slips secrets in my ear. I smell the people I knew as a child—I smell them in their tombs.

"I didn't do anything!" a spirit cries.

The city drifts by in its sorrowful regalia. The end is already present, whole. I don't need weapons to bring it down. We merge. I bask in patience. I spread through the cold night. My saying voice is turned off.

He sings.

My other soul remembers.

Our knowing is big with dream—everyone feels it. Our lights turn on at the same time.

My heart is without poems. Its train drags through the mud. Is there a new way of writing? Is there a new way of suffering?

Sunlight on my wrinkled hands. The young man plays his guitar, his dark wrists turning like rivers. I dawdle on the bridge, having no preference for either bank.

Patrick with his molten heart plays a music no one has paid for, no one owns. Loss stalks down the block, up to her night-gowned hips in our spilled youth.

A woman can never hold. A woman can never be held. Love is only a shipwreck.

Easter Sunday comes twining her hair, comes loping, drunken through the fog. A helicopter seed, tiny, veined, like an aborted child, on the porch. The music has no teeth, just gums. India calls to me in dream-language.

In the white, neon colors. Fever makes me spare, experimental. Heat swims in my arms, down my back. I'm finally warm enough; this is the warmth I was missing. Head full of holly and blue knives.

The French lady peers over her balcony, wearing a blue feather headdress, hands on her hips. Dorian looks at herself in the mirror. Women in floppy hats and pastel dresses, men in seersucker suits drift by like paddle boats. The mystery is disguised in holiday. The poverty is pinned with taffeta.

The souls are bobbed and fluffed. A man in a cowboy hat and Mardi Gras beads looks down Royal Street, a cigarette burning between his fingers.

I watch them walking with their beers and Irish coffees, holding flowers by their stems, their legs covered and uncovered, each one connected closely or loosely to the beast. I look, but I can't see their suffering—it is embedded in their peace.

It's resurrection day. "Happy Easter" on the lips of the people. A girl's hair grows like a river to her waist. Where is the girl? Where is the river?

Dorian fans her mother. They play "Sweet Georgia Brown." Heartbreaking people sit on the curb—country people with frowzy hair and walking shoes. Young people pause on their bikes to chat. I see them becoming old, their styles going out of style. The people carry something—or something carries them—like trolley cars connected to invisible lines. They are automatic. So am I.

Then, they look at me with knowing eyes, eyes with their shades open, as if I were real. They surprise me with their beauty, with their qualities. They are so much themselves, plain, like babies in bathtubs. Women check their reflections in windows. Men film the scene, their eyes like God's. Children whine, buck-toothed and grotesque.

A young man walks down the street. But the street also gives rise to the young man; at no point is there a young man, and at no point is there not a young man. He is part of the street, an expression of its life.

Afternoon has a different character. It's meaner, more of a lunatic, more materialistic than the morning. By now, we forget our dreams. The day broods, by turns steamy and cool. It is April.

In the night I lay awake. I play the harp of Sandiman—his skin, his voice, his myth. Wind chimes rake hungrily over my consciousness. There is nothing ahead—just the world.

Patrick sings on the corner alone. His song is as beautiful as the ocean. It is the measure of beauty. It knocks other walls of beauty out of place, widens the chasm beauty can fill. A wave sweeps over my mind—it is bigger than he is, blue-eyed and hatted with his yellow guitar case before him on the slate tiles.

Money is coming to take me away
to pour all my drinks and pull on my braids
to give me what none of my lovers could give
some nectar to strain through the holes of this sieve

Money is coming to mate with my soul
and we'll make a baby who'll never grow old
and we'll make museums of our malnourished hearts
and melt ourselves down and be sold for our parts

Money is coming to ruin our dreams
to burn up the lawns and sew up our seams
money is coming to kill all the pain
and write us an epitaph where we are lain

2

I drive in the cold rain past Pearl River, cypresses, a long ribbon of sandy beach. A sea of marsh grasses cradles my heart. Wind in cypress and palm. I taste the water: salty. It moves quickly, in dark green curves, different from Mississippi water. I remember my last look at the river, lit lavender under power lines in a pink sky.

I arrive on the island in the frenzied night. It's too hot to sleep in the car beside the public housing projects. The inn is full. Bob Herb takes me in for the night. In the morning I sit mournfully beside him in a bar with a swimming-pool.

In the blinding sunlight the bartender pours alcohol into plastic cups. The bar-back dumps ice into a trough. Swim-suited customers pull credit cards out of wallets. On a flat-screen TV, a woman bites rapturously into a sandwich.

Questions roam around in me like ghosts in dead-end hallways. My body pulses. The highway shakes. The sea trembles. The souls of people blink on and off behind their eyes. Confusion and grief become part of a general purring, an infinite orchestra. I write in lines, but the truth is an explosion. I can't trick the truth; it will come out one way or another.

I set up the typewriter beneath a sign: "Fresh Produce." People drift in drunken flocks over the painted white lines of the crosswalk. Andy, a young veteran, is living in a tall beer can in the landscaping of the church. A wealthy man tells me he used to talk to God alone at the back of the ship, nights in the middle of the sea.

A young woman is lying unconscious on a church pew, her long skirt softly draped over her body. Tommy gathers her and carries her inside. I sleep in a closet while a man and woman scream at one another in the hallway.

I change my clothes on Angela Street, under the trees. Boats don't leave from here, they say. You've come to the wrong place. Keep looking.

Leila names her troubles beside the ocean as if she is counting beads. If you listen, we are all inside this music.

What kinds of keys are twirling in my eyes? I recall under the stars that I am big, big. I hear myself, I feel myself like a tongue of flame. We are more than we suppose. An old woman passes. Her curves are soft. Her back hurts. Inside, she is as omnipresent, as strident as the weather.

Doves cross my path when I am happy, and doves cross my path when I am sad. Leaves insist, converting the elements into themselves. A city of slaves—and those who drive them are also slaves. My heart circles, looking for something it lost. The world rips my mask from my face. The town chokes me; I wilt.

I learn the hiding places of the homeless, the seamy brown of their faces in the whispering morning. At a hotel on the beach, European families emerge from white bedsheets. As much as the horizon is a symbol, the men on the sofa are symbols—of the entire truth. The tongue of fire dancing in me is a symbol. Everything we can see is a portrait of the whole which we cannot see.

The preacher talks of Jesus calming the storm.

"You must search for that compass that points in the same direction, no matter what's happening."

Tiny yards, tiny gardens—a vague despair. Other times flicker through the streets. I prod myself: what am I? How am I? The street is suspended in the sky. Emptiness in the eyes of the passersby. They hobble, stumble toward death. They know it. Even in their joy, they are afraid. Patiently, making themselves comfortable, they journey toward their stiffening. Today, my dead feet peeked out of the blue water. Death is always here. Still, we try to get dollars. Andy fights with his new girlfriend in the churchyard.

I am weighted with the gifts I bear. I trudge between shades. I change color, but I don't change heart. The wind swears—I will have to go soon, go soon. What is the feeling I have hunted for words to name—the death in the closets of the atoms, in the back rooms of the mind?

Pain—but only English pain. Nothing behind the words.

Beds of leaves go to sleep on the sidewalk. Homeless humans look for shade. Falling leaves don't look for anything—they go with the wind, headlong.

My heart sleeps far under the circus of words—their somersaults, fireworks. My course is lit like writing in dark water. I sleep while I seem to be awake.

"I need you," I say to no one as I walk the candy streets. I sleep like a fallen flower on the public beach.

Humanity shows through the prison bars, stripes of light in a shaded jungle. Eternity lowers her eyelids, lets us go on with our innocent folly.

Watch them go headlong into their tragedies. They hide behind their forms. Their truth is refracted, projected into dimension. Two-legged fruit, the seed hidden. They cross the street in clothes fresh from the racks. The night carries its shoes in its hand. I look for one to love, but none of them are he. Then I see him behind each pair of eyes. We disappear. Our words blanch and scar in the weather.

Alex juggles in the street, handsome, shirtless. He has walked across America, hiding in plain sight, sleeping in suburban lawns.

I say with certainty, "I will find my boat tonight."

At the harbor, evening is in the water, rippling in squares. A lime slice floats. A fishing boat moves. My veins stand up. Seagulls drift poignantly through the evening. A storm is coming. There is nothing to find.

I stay with Boris in the unfinished room and watch his endless card tricks. His eyes look in two directions at once.

Gabilan says Boris is a suicide.

"Gabilan is a sacred clown," Boris says.

In the day I work for Gabilan, sanding, mudding, painting. Gabilan teases me, calls me "Poet." Fena brings us food at midday.

He steps into the sidewalk, stopping me. He doesn't tell me his name. He calls himself "us." Others call him Inaru. He points out the electric lines running under the streets, the sewage system, the paved roads.

"We're here in the USA, aren't we?"

He is from a place I haven't thought of before.

He alights on his winged tricycle, eyes wild, ringed in kohl. He cuts with the cutlass while he holds the coconut in the other hand.

What does it feel like? A palm, opening. I crumble like red earth. People in the street: full of empty space. Between their atoms, howling windows of shadow.

"I'm sorry," some say.

"I'm not sorry," others say.

We have broken something beautiful, all of us, together. On the corner, an old man plays cover songs on an electric guitar. His dog sits before him, wearing a pair of sunglasses. People take pictures, leave a tip.

Our minds swim like fish in a single ocean: they hang at various depths. Suicides, sacred clowns, a love that's always just around the corner.

In the morning, the sun tears transients from their hiding places, along with the other secrets of the night. But still he hides in this garland of daylight, strung by darknesses of waning hope.

A small man with a violin asks permission to recite a poem. I listen to his verses about a love who fills the world with light.

"That's all," he says. "That's what struck me when I saw you. That's a poem by Giacomo Leopardi. He had a tragic life, man."

He scoffs, kicks his foot. I reach out for his hand, but he shrinks away, in terror of being touched. I put $10 in the violin case at his feet. His eyes darting, he picks the bill up with a handkerchief and puts it into his pocket.

Many call this place a paradise, but it's another hell. Many hells dwell within it.

But Leila says, "Sometimes this tree has yellow blossoms all over it."

I get a funny feeling. It's as if the place were touching me, trying to tell me something with its fingertips.

"Nothing matters," I say.

What I mean is that the nuance is endless. There is nothing to indicate.

Alex and I walked across the island and out into the water, where the neon lights of a gaudy hotel spread down the surface of black tide. The moon did tricks with the edges of the clouds. We sat, each with our sadness. Alex's sadness was like my own—wordless, and almost without hope.

Pain in one's foot. Pain in another's stomach. Pain in another one's head. Pain crawls over the streets, looking for fuel. I know it, because it has been in me. Pain opens a little door. Inside doesn't talk to outside. There is a rift.

Inaru sprays neem and water, spreads sheets. He washes our feet from the tap on the side of a hotel. He feels my cheeks with the back of his hand, like a jug of water he is checking for temperature. He waters the plants on the porch of the abandoned house, as if quelling demons. They are Gabriela's plants, and he has let them die.

People with faces of mountains, faces of illness, faces of poverty. Inaru climbs a tree and drops mangoes to a man below. People stop and look at him, up high. He cooks a big pot and people come to eat. They ask him for money: "Let me hold something." He gives money to all who ask.

He ties up a mosquito net in someone's back yard. In the morning he digs at his teeth with a twig. He stands on the truck and pulls Trinidad cherries from the bush. Beside the water he finds a coconut and opens it with his teeth.

I am unable to fit into any groove. I peter out. I have stopped becoming. I have gone again into the wastelands, where no one will hear my cries. So much distance can't be translated. Thinking passes below the horizon.

Andy sits beside me and cries. His brother has been killed in Afghanistan. He has been drunk for three days and hasn't stopped talking. Now he is silent and wet with tears.

From above, I watch the rain-soaked clowns, their face-paint running down, inky-black. I rise over the shoulders of the trains, out over the billboards, disappearing, like a childhood dream.

In the haunted closeness of the island, the leaves and trunks are packed tightly into miniature constructions. Everything screams under a thin layer of handiness.

I smell old things in the rain. Flowers bobble on a branch in the downpour. What do they mean?

"Let's do it again," the raindrops say.

Things happen like a cloth stretched over a drum—the truth is in the empty space, but the noise is in its covering, its mask. I love one person as I ought to love them all.

In the hearts of those who have suffered and grown wise, fallen leaves cover up the foolish monuments. No one has time now for plaques or horsemen. The world has moved on.

Sadness lies between us, like people who meet in a dream. Here I hold this bouquet of nothing, in a doorway I will never pass through.

"The trees are growing up," Mr. Chapman says. "Why are we all looking down?"

In a place beyond the city lights, old ways of thinking undress, go to sleep beside the water. Some part of me has been pulled up by the root. There is no need to go back tracing. The whole story is here, on its knees.

White fallen flowers turn transparent on the wet sidewalk, begin to blend with everything. Keep Out, reads the doorstep, succinctly, in store-bought letters. One white flower lies like a mouth against the well-sealed floorboard. The fallen blossoms are not rotting, they are giving way to the world.

The goodness I meant to usher in is pig-faced. The new words are asleep with the old words, like drunken lovers, not sure who is who. The typewriter table is broken and taped and broken again. I leave a tiny mandala in every place I touch. This garden stings and hisses, sparkles with webs of loss.

We have to suffer to become ourselves. The suffering is pointing at something right now, but I keep looking at its finger. I must shed this way of saying, of moving. My dreams scratch at their sheath, but the sheath doesn't break.

Something happens on another plane. We dance it out like marionettes, like shadow-puppets—we cover up the truth with our lives.

I am raining, now, but in another moment I am gathering. I am raining, here, but in another place I am finished raining.

The violinist stops me as I pass him. He sings a Spanish ballad in a reedy voice, stomping with one foot to keep time. He was adopted by Catholics whom he hates bitterly. He talks with his bow in his hand, resting it in his crook of his neck.

My mind makes no noise. It is caught like a cat picking through a rosebush. The schizophrenic on the bench looks for his next victim. My love hangs like a bead of water on the edge of a leaf. Uncertainty spreads out its colorful tail. I am alone among the humans. Do I see myself anywhere? In the flying birds lit from below in the evening. In the slow movement of the palms.

Moments pass, holding up their skirts from the wet pavement. I wonder to find myself still in a city. Dreariness climbs over me like an infant, clutching my skin and hair.

Everyone is turned inward, their ears pressed to the hollow mound of themselves. They are frantic, hearing the soft moaning of a mother-beast within, giving birth to the end.

"Do you have a plan for yourself?" Gabilan asks.

There is only a way of being for the moment. It casts a shadow, so I know it is not perfect.

Foreboding is the evening shadow, and regret is the shadow of the morning.

Can I get low enough to cast no shadow at all? Only then will I find life—when I expect nothing.

"When you feel impure and separate, it is because you have not been patient," Rumi says.

Inaru changes shape like a character in a dream.

Like water for the thirsty, or like a mother curing her infant of its newness, what passes between us is not ours to give. It floods.

The earth withholds its kindness. On the other side of joy I sit, an empty shell in the cool night. Sorrow-full, swollen with pain where before expectation stretched the skin. Is this the way it will always be?

Inaru hasn't come with the night. I grow poor. Love wheels its object through the tourist strip. The world will change, somehow. But who will help it?

"You help by example," Gabilan said. "By pure example."

I am in my own shadow.

"I am not nothing!" a voice in me cries.

So I still have to learn to be nothing.

"You hurt me," my heart says to no one—perhaps it speaks to itself. I am here to support those I meet, not the other way around.

One look back: a vine-laden forest floor, clean of small growth in the shade. Both severe and grand, it needs no ornament. It is draped elegantly in its solitude. Secretly, I blow a batch of lilies tiny to bloom later underfoot. And now I go, quick-throated as the rainbow, to where I'm needed.

Women are the ones holding the keys—but they don't care about open or closed, out or in. They are busy somewhere finer and more dangerous.

The world keeps turning, getting sick with confusion, thinking it's the only thing that's real. I want to remove the petals from its eyes. But it's not time. Inside, it's still mottled flesh, not even close to being ready to die.

"I'm hurt," my stupid heart keeps saying, when I take my hand from its mouth. I have to tell it again and again the way things are.

I am as bad as the rest of them, flailing, poisoned, through the streets. I choke on them, on how much I love them, need them, want them to stay. The light keeps changing: green yellow red. Humans flow over the corner like a snow drift. How I miss them!

I can't see through my costume. My people are straggling. It's pointless to try to advance them. We are like gift-shop toys. We are dead already.

My attachment clatters like pool balls breaking. It swishes like pines in the wind. It is shed in little pieces, in little pieces it softens the ground. A moment ago, I knew everything. Now, I cut my knowing open and bleed it.

Can I go unarmed through one more moment? People practice dying like a Christmas pageant. They walk sideways and as if they had just grown tall. The prophets wag their tongues. The end wears too much jewelry. Broken something beautiful, chants my heart.

The true activity is not the activity that requires conniving. The true activity cannot be helped.

"Why do you need a destination?" Sandiman asked.

In a corner where many drunks have peed, I share the

cinder blocks with a headless, soggy bird. The parking lot is crossed by a flock of dry leaves.

My dreams come up for air, but today's sorrows push them down by the crown of their heads; they drown.

I can see, by looking at Inaru's shadow, what the light must have been. I came too late to see it burning. It can be seen in the faces of those who love him. But what is in his face?

I feel so many things, but how to say them?

I smell Richard on the wind
His saffron eyes his paper skeleton
that good man leaking swallows
good man leaking violins

I'm standing outside of the old church now
the old church I never did burn her down
I'm outside but I won't go in
They say pretty darling pretty darling where you been

I see Richard in the evening
it's a red light for the one who's always leaving
a good man with a pool of blood beneath him
why are all the good men always leaking

My baby with the cathedral eyes
played the black keys and he played the white
I sang as sweetly as I could
I left the street and took the woods

I feel Richard in the spin
the earth's beginning to end again
I loved you one I loved you all
but Richard held me like a wrecking ball

My baby the one with the music box
up all night with the equinox
the rain poured out her silver applause
emptied her wallet for a worthy cause

And Richard's walking through my dreams
hunting him a one-eyed suicide queen
the colonies are cracked beneath his feet
the trees have left the woods and took the street

The plaza's empty the gallows are full
it's a brown girl's skull for our crowning jewel
and all the songs we never sung
will leave their footprints on our tongue

3

Nothingness all over me, beating its wings. I wanted to move by sea, but in the sky again, I look down on tiny boats below.

From above, I see the world. This way, I don't have to see myself.

Rain and darkness, the streets empty except for drivers standing beside parked taxis, people sleeping on cardboard in doorways. A light here and there in a bar.

I don't know how to be without system, like the pigeons and the falling seeds that perforate the business day.

This heat is different from the heat I've left behind. My heart beats green with the sea.

The city doesn't notice me. She is wrapped up in herself. The walls loom like girls with secrets, dressed in soft colors. They cover their lips with their fingers. A mystery is reflected in the blind glass, in the nests of the transients, in the light rain.

On one side lies the bay, deep blue, sleeping. On the other side, the sea fights with the shore. I have seen this, though I do not know what it means to say, "I have seen this." I have seen the sea play among rocks below a cemetery full of stone angels—the saddest stone angels I have ever seen. They dangle garlands of stone flowers over the beds of the dead. It is the same mistake as always. Some of their garlands are broken. Some of their arms have fallen off.

Aguacero: the word appears on the lips of passersby,

like a puddle white with sky, a flower I have just learned to recognize. Ice-cream sellers roll carts, ring bells. Pigeons pick between stones. I search for the entrance into brown eyes drifting by inside brown faces. The people are soft and below the horizon. Their minds glitter like lakes in a desert.

Beside the cathedral, a blind man shakes coins in a plastic cup. He is leaning, doubled-over, on a cane. Pedestrians cross themselves as they pass the church. A bride descends the stone stairs. People cheer, take pictures, get in cars and drive away. The blind man shakes his cup.

Deep spaces sculpt the form. Silence punctuates the sound. Under the hush of shame, deafening applause. The quiet is bitten by the crying of a pigeon.

The city's angels give me shelter, plastic spoons, cigarettes. But they are motionless, like the angels of stone, suspended endlessly in the gesture of mourning.

Life gathers over emptiness; time passes, leaving no trace. A young man crosses the beach folding the palm flowers he sells in the streets. He carries his death in his backpack across the sand.

Like amnesiacs, empty buildings repeat their names. A palsied lantern lights and goes out.

"Cuidate allí," says an ice-cream seller. He smiles with a mouth full of gold.

I sing alone on the rooftop. A young man jumps down from the sky.

"America is a big One-Eye," he says. "Have you heard of the New World Order?"

He's nineteen, from Senegal. He is very black, but his

cheeks blush pink. He too is an angel.

We look at each other, as if we could see by looking. I watch as Inaru performs miracles. He climbs the sea grape tree and shakes the fruits down for me to gather. I give him everything at once, as if our lives have already passed, whole.

In forested hills I am mute, but my heart makes a desperate noise. A tree cries green mango tears. The evening opens up its many throats.

"Lost-him" is the seed which the hard, green pulp conceals. Time clings to the seed, but it will turn soft and disappear.

Ghosts walk through me, sit beside me, touch my arm, my cheek. Darkness bleeds into the landscape like ink through a napkin. Everywhere I look, death takes off her mask. Atoms crowd around, trying to design me. I want to send them in baskets down the river. A puppy chews my finger. We are both already in our graves.

Although I see Inaru, he is already far away. I see the hearts of those who have loved him, so many torches blown out on the road.

The coquís make a music like leaves being carried by a river. Clouds cover and uncover the half-moon. There are faces in the clouds, trees, and hills.

Pío speaks of plagues, Revelations.

"We have less than twelve months to get ready."

"How do we prepare?"

"The only preparation is spiritual preparation. Otherwise, what? You want to live a few more weeks than the others?"

Half the population of Puerto Rico has cancer. Pío is

saving seeds for the coming scarcity.

The city thrashes like a wild beast. Perhaps it's true there is no more time for gentleness. But how to be sure? The only way to be sure is to be no one at all.

I go on being, though much time is lost. My soul has held its silence long, but still utters no word. The blind man shakes his cup. I hear somewhere a music, but it's muffled, echoing. My mind whips like a hose. Pigeons pick between the bricks. I worry for the humans. They hold maps, cameras, keys. They teeter on steps.

The afternoon becomes soft. Machines grate by, sleek and ferocious. They make meaningless the harmony and the subtlety, the efforts of the monks.

The skies are occupied, pierced by army planes. Our eyes, too, have been neutralized.

Half-god, half-crazy. My fear mixes with his fear. I love like someone tending to a corpse.

The silence is bitten by the crying of a pigeon.

My love takes the boxes from the rooms. I am here with the pigeons. Here with the flies, the dry leaves, and the worst of the city. There is the saxophone and a constant whisper of electricity.

It's raining in my heart. Saints of stone look toward el Morro.

I still believe in the terrible beauty underneath this frozen present.

At the back of the graveyard, a door is open. I lay my cheek against the cement doorway. Later, as if waking, I walk through, down to the shore.

The tide resolves itself against the rocks: nothing is left out. I read stories in the surf. I have long felt my mind tainted, but even the taint is inside the mind. All things are.

Yes, the secrets are known, but not by me, nor by the sea. They are known by knowing. How else could it be?

"No te salves," breathes the roaring ocean.

The fort by night: wet moon on mown lawn, planed walls of stone, the sea wide, carrying a foggy blue light.

"This place is very strong," Augustin says. "You can feel the water crazy all around you, but you are still."

He names poets and educators, heroes who have fallen into the cemetery by the sea. He is a constellation, his eyes smooth and black as river stones. He talks of the meetings of a few that decide the fate of the world, of fertility experiments performed on Puerto Rican women without their knowledge.

"This information is available," he says, "but they have succeeded in their program to make us ignorant."

Police men drink coffee in Plaza Colón. They salute me: "Buenos." Lionel walks with me through La Perla. It was here they sent the crazy people, the lepers and prostitutes, outside the city wall. In his kitchen, Lionel has made a sunset of paper clouds and string.

Julius moves his skeleton puppet. His daughter makes chalk drawings on the sidewalk.

Clank of silverware. The night going to sleep.

The clock hands always point to twelve on the Banco Popular. The electric lines are elegant as swans. A pile of conch shells goes to sleep on the rooftop. The tropical clouds are smooth over Easter morning.

"Hay que ponerte fuerte," says Radamés.

We are the fantasies of a burning fever. The roses are passing by. Civilians bless me. Wincing at invisible attacks, I walk in strips of shade.

Ripples pass over and through one another like ghosts. The bald woman who showers at the bus stop.

The abandoned city, heavy with beauty, crawling with vines. Armed guards, weeping pigeons. A scrap of a dream I've stepped into.

"Just let go," Gabilan says.
I read my poem to Gabilan.
"Sepulcro?" he repeats, incredulous.

These hands came from the others. There is no one to defend you from yourself. Today I am human. I can only think of love. The blue is blue in the sky so blue. Heavy cords of earthliness. I walk along the shadows. Promises are hidden in crumbling courtyards, regrets fall heavily in the hot sunlight. The clouds are eloquent, take a deep bow. The city is talking in its sleep—it doesn't want to wake up. Good, kind faces.

I speak to strangers in the streets of San Juan.

"I'm knocking on the door of my soul," I say, "but she doesn't want anything to do with it—"

"Why? Since when?" Bartolome insists.

"I died."

"That's not good enough. You must ask yourself: what would you fight for, what would you die for? Then you must do it."

A day of incredible pain. I can hardly speak. I walk forlorn, looking for something. I walk to the fort with Augustin.

"I'm lost," I say.

"It's time for you to be happy," he says. The words are happy to be in his mouth. The weight, you have to learn to let it go. Kneel down and touch your head to Pachamama if you are humble. Forget your conscience. What does your heart tell you?"

I go hurrying through the sea glass, passing hermit crabs and strange rocks. I am powerful. I sing. I rush. I make fists. I want to send treasures. I have found them in myself.

Suddenly, I'm sick. I'm tired. I'm in pain.

Bare necks in the jewelry store window—headless, bodiless necks, bare of gems for the night.

I dreamed there was an empire, that its tanks and missiles lay on the beaches. I dreamed of helicopters and jets in the sky.

Dreamy, dreary saxophone notes in the galleries of a vacant downtown. There is no one to tell. I walked with the flowers and the stars and the moon. I walked with the palms and the porches and the lights.

I'm the only one who can see the setting sun, this dream born a captive, born condemned.

My face cries. Tears strike over my face. Yet stillness inside, the words, "All is well." Something is broken, but not me. I have grown tall.

Under a full moon on the airport road I sit, listening to bullfrogs and my own incessant blood. In a place that is almost always still, there is a leaning. I spread out through the landscape.

Georgetown is toothless and cock-eyed, mad with heat and poverty, walking on three legs. The streets are full of ghosts and mosquito coils. Factories spill poison smells.

Inaru's house, the tree that grows in his placenta. His cousin, Christ-like—I cannot understand him when he speaks. An old woman complains that her floor is rotting. She worked all her life in the sugarcane fields.

Inaru fixes bicycles he has shipped from the land of riches and gives them to the villagers. Young men gather, listen to him patiently. They know nothing will come of his talk. Still, it has the warmth of their fathers' and grandfathers' voices. It stirs them with closeness and distance: the closeness of blood, the distance of the grave.

He acts with mercy and without mercy—for he is in the world, unapologetic, and will do it, whatever it may be. But gently, he will do it, like one slitting the throat of an animal—neatly, with his tongue curled over his teeth.

Far down a mud road, the bricks of the old refinery are

turning to dust in the earth. Where the tree hangs over the water, someone was hanged. Hanged for the crime of loving a white woman, though the love, like the sweetness from the earth, was coerced. Inaru is familiar with the ghosts of both parties, but they don't appear to us today.

In the bus, a mother mouths her infant's cheeks. We change buses amid sound systems and colorful umbrellas. At the water's edge Inaru uproots a coconut sprout and breaks it into pieces.

"Happy international day of the woman," he says.

We motor through swaths of darkness. A heavy rain. The trees loom and gesture. The motor stalls. The flashlight fails. We turn in circles in the darkness. The jungle opens into marsh. Sunil paddles. Lotus flowers stretch toward the moon, open-mouthed like baby birds. We reach a round house of wood and thatch. The woman inside pours tea like a master.

Trees reflect on still water, casting intricate symmetrical shapes, like traveling through a kaleidoscope. I become still. The motor dies. Inaru and Sunil paddle through the channel and across the wide, grey river. Stars emerge in an enormous sky. I am alone, deeply hidden in myself. Near the city, golden shore lights tumble down the water. I am outside of time, finally. Finally, I have left home.

Everything recedes—the birds in the sky, the ripples in the water, the lines of the rooftops, the shapes in the clouds. They flap their wings. "Goodbye," they cry. They throw their bags over their shoulders.

"You must be brave," I tell myself, but I feel small. Then,

after all, I am big enough. Nothing touches me. The world is like vapor. Fear itself is the poetry. Fear itself is the glass eye in the palm of the hand.

The village climbs into my eyes. I see the years like a veil trailing behind: sore, painted shutters in a cement wall, the trees Inaru planted, now tall.

The sky is full of swan feathers. Children speak, but I don't understand them. I look in the mirror, but I don't see myself. I change shape. Am I beautiful or ugly? I don't know. Chickens croak. I am too small to contain all I contain.

The sun rises. Inaru sweeps the mosquito net open. He wheezes, coughs. He plants trees in the yard. He mutters about the cement. He tries to kill a river of ants with kerosene and fire.

My gaze is like a spotlight, pointing at nothing.

Something has passed between us, has changed hands subtly. What it is, I still don't know, but it is complete.

Drawing closer, I find myself at a greater distance. The space between things has merely increased. I'm left alone with the power lines, slipping away. The sounds of birds and of Inaru plucking plastic strings are just colors cut by the moving surface of the water.

Things have less meaning than before, not more. Every day, the world becomes emptier. Soon, I suppose, there will be nothing.

Hindi music warbles over the sounds of chickens and cows. Neighbors drift and wait for orders. Inaru washes clothes in a bucket in the yard. I look in the mirror.

"The heart doesn't make mistakes," I tell myself.

But here is the mosquito net he swept away, leaving me

alone at dawn. Since dawn, I have been alone.

He recounts the ways in which he was broken. Political violence, death. He wanted to bury the dead and resurrect the truth. His blood kin tried to kill him with poison. In the jungle he purged with mystical plants and lived. Since then, exile. The true path like a dead limb he could never sever.

The lights are on along the strip
of cafes people ride inside like ships
I am towing close behind
but my heart does not turn on its light

The past seems so far away
all the places I have loved have changed
was I a child frightened by the waves
or a watchman who just couldn't stay awake

Was I a lover on a train or a twirler of flames
a painter in a basement all alone
was I an exile before the suitcase and the door
I don't know anymore what is home

The piano I once played no longer tunes
the house where I once stayed, they say it's haunted
and the island is a siren turned to stone
in a sea of forgetting what I wanted

The sea itself, or just its solitude
love, or a lover all my own
and did I really hope for revolution
or did I merely have to throw a stone

All the lines that I sold, did I write them for gold
now the lines in the earth show it's changing
but if my devils come in to give my angels a spin
I know they'll leave again if I'm patient

My empty bag is hanging up outside
my stories scattered all along the road
and I am feeling dizzy from the wine
sealed up when I stopped here long ago

The future blossoms out of us like birds
grown up but still clinging to the nest
they are made for somewhere far beyond
and they'll leave one by one when they are ready

But if the one that I choose takes the winding road
and I take the straight one to the sea
will she ever arrive, will she look to the horizon
will she wash her green eyes of their dreaming

4

London is bare, its buildings without eyelids, without eyelashes. A flock of moths taking off, revealing the thing they have been eating. Inside the flesh, the bones are white. Inside the bones, the universe is repeated.

In a market outside the train station, Abbas gives me dates, mango, falafel, coffee.

"We are both angels," he says, "and devils too. But we try to only show the angel, and to minimize the devil. Everyone is the same."

He plays classical music on his small FM radio. He rolls a spliff.

"My wife and my life," he says, gazing at it. The light is fluid and delirious, swimming in the window.

We walk above the city. I clutch the deep English grass between my knuckles.

A blue-winged shadow on my thirsty heart. I sleep beside the river, covered in Abbas's coat. On the bridge beside the river, I speak with a Greek book-seller: old, hopelessly old. He gives me a painting, coffee. He sends me to Montmartre.

The people touch the earth with their feet. Gentle animals again, they are returned to their simplicity. Though they are also bad, they are good above the city, surrounded by their own rings, like swans on water.

A cold night gets closer. The places I have been gather in me, swell my skin. I grow in fear, grow cold inside. For every day there is a new kind of suffering.

A voice in me calls out for mercy: "Please don't let it hurt too much."

The cry is old and has been in other mouths than mine.

Massimo picks me up at the border. He feeds me olives, sparkling water. I don't know how to say in Italian, "You are an angel."

We drive through valleys with mud-colored houses in their crevasses. The sea is made tall by the mountains. Olive trees shimmer silver in strong winds. Yellow butterflies die on the windshield.

The sky faces the hills, depth at its back. Earth and sea keep their depths within. Where the two depths meet, humans have their being.

I sit in Oreana's garden under a tree full of lemons. I have been lost in designs for my own happiness. Now I remember the joke: I am not so small.

The self appears in deep, silent places, where you wouldn't expect it, manipulating things. If I stop believing in myself, who do I become? Who watches these doings?

When I am free of self, I am noble, I overflow. But the self is afraid: those who go beyond the city walls will have to defend themselves—the army won't help.

Dimitris reads my face like tea leaves. "You are wonderful!" he laughs, breathless, doubling over.

The sea ripples. Schools of fish drift close to the rock, hunting. My eyes settle on a minnow. A fish darts and swallows it whole. I am made of this.

Looking for happiness in the world of illusion—that is the problem. Here, any victory is for only for a moment. Above the village, ancient groves of olive trees, dark and twisting, with eyes under the earth.

They talk of revolution, of the arsenals on Crete. Athena works in the café in the morning. Dimitris tends the bar at night. He doesn't collect money. They have to hide it in his pockets, in the drawers.

Sadness stalks into the landscape. I recognize her, hunched over, her fingers curled around her robes.

Suicide rises up—not as an act, but as a frequency, a color that fills the sky, a storm, its edges blurred, a song whose words are "No, no, no."

"We want to be free, free, free," Dimitris says.

"Who knows what will happen in November," they say.

"We think something is going to happen."

But while we have our candy world, our cappuccinos, how can there be cessation?

A day is fading. Sparrows chase one another on the power lines. The sparrows know not past and future; they live as in a dream.

A woman waters marigolds. No division between perceiver and perceived.

The story of the self repeats, while the body dissolves around it.

The lights are on along the strip of cafes, their heartbeats gently amplified. My heart keeps its toes in the water. My heart does not turn on its light.

I grow invisible and profoundly lost. The marigolds are still here. They have existed since yesterday, and still, they exist.

I remember sorrows like old friends: a town I loved that changed. The fear-time has gone on long. Good and evil see through one another's eyes. The end grows tired on the road, sits down in an old church. She starts to dream, forgets where she was going.

Moments take down their hair, wash their feet. They rub the makeup from their round green eyes.

My noises rise up like the sounds of birds with the sun. It has been a long night. I have rested. I have dreamed.

"You were born for the work of the mind," Dimitris says.

Olive trees, more than a hundred years old, stretch into the sky. Spotlights diffuse over the company's faces. Mosquito coils unfurl spools of smoke in the grass. The family wine is placed near the most important visitor. The hostess stands to touch her glass to each guest's glass. The host walks the bowl of bread all the way around the table.

I walk through the grove. I touch the olive tree. I exist as if between the stitches of life, not on one plane or another, but in the space between things, in eternity.

Women walk in the street with their children. Girls sell roses wrapped in cellophane. You can smell them when they pass. I ask Dante to take me sailing with him to Sardegna, but he leaves without me. Dimitris asks me to stay, but I will go.

The truth is hidden. Smoke wreaths the beings, desolate in the insistent daylight. The evening will take a long time yet. I think I hear drums, but it is just construction—destruction.

The sky is bluing. People move, their feet pushing insistently against the stone. Everything is emptied.

My body flies in every direction, a flock dispersing. The words write themselves, carrying the soul along like a fish in a net. Like schools of fish, the people move, one eye on their prey. They dart here and there, seeking satisfaction, permanence. Pigeons reflect the righteous greed of humans in terms of simple hunger. The reflections in shop windows are not quite shadow, not quite light.

Each table contains love as deep as an ocean, but the love is brittle at the edges, rubs against those around it. Men and women jiggle prayer beads behind their backs. Do they see God?

Night stretches out and breathes. People glide over the streets. Time stops. Glasses float on trays like ghosts. A waiter steps out of his body. He is pure soul, struggling to exist.

A woman makes her way around the tables, holding out her hand. Everyone looks to either side, ignores her. A bearded man sits on the ground with his hand open. He growls like an animal and mutters to himself. People pass him by, eating ice cream.

The street gets drunk, becomes overly expressive. Women pass in the fullness of their beauty—but their beauty is useless to protect them.

A girl passes, her ice-blue eyes framed in lashes thickly

painted with mascara. She moves through her beauty like a panther through a jungle.

Women stand on legs heavy like fruit.

This is how things are: full of themselves.

Peddlers launch twirling lights above the tree-tops. A shop-owner holds a freddo cappuccino in a domed plastic cup. I see musicians, I even hear their bells, but I am far away. Hopelessness pulls my hands down to my sides. The future opens like a wound.

An old man leans on a cane in a doorway. Purple hatches from the blue in the sky. I cannot say what has entered me. A young man walks slowly down the street, playing a kazoo and a guitar. Music trills. Spinning toys fall through the air. Hopelessness sits beside me, letting her hair lift in the current. It is sad to reach the end of a road, to see the scenery closing all around.

Do they smell my lack? But I do not lack for words tonight. I am clean as a washed baby. I am clear. It is hopelessness who jams my joints, but I love her so much, I know she will turn into hope. Something unlooked-for will happen. It has to be this way.

The women are like skies full of stars. An older couple looks at the sky. They can't make anything of it—because they are in it. I lie in this room, drowning in time. I feel useless, I say. It is all I can say. Tell me, tell me, Dimitris repeats. But I cannot tell.

The past unravels any time it is pulled. Misery weighs heavily upon these walkers on the earth. I can hear the songs of women I've known—we are all one river of song, the song of not having been loved in the right way. Women pass by in their full beauty, but it is useless. They cannot defend themselves against their losses. Things were different once—the old people remind us. Now everything that was opened closes again.

I need the truth to come closer, where I can see it.

No one can see what is inside me. I look into the black eyes of Athena. She is more beautiful than anything—than anything.

Hope washes over me like cool water. Things change, hatch out of themselves. Love swirls around me. Oh, my people! They are gorgeous and good. They are what they are supposed to be. At the same time, they are unfortunate. My heart shakes like a piece of paper—I am one of them, and I know. It hurts. It hurts.

I see people walking, their hearts beating in their chests, pain and pleasure swimming through their skin. It isn't a gesture, a dream. It is real. The street is terrible, terribly real. The young musicians play sweetly, but it is too much, now. Writing seems false—as if I needed proof.

New Orleans blooms in my mind like a magician's flower: bending weeds in orange sunset, train tracks and factories. Dogs roam the old town. Children tap on my keys. It grows more difficult, instead of becoming easier. The moment won't take off its old eye patch. Our dirges roll around like ferris wheels.

Panic runs down me like water through a river bed. Each

person unrolls his packet of tobacco in the morning light. They do not remember that they are real. Not one of their faces shows an inkling of it. It's like sitting in a room full of ghosts, knowing that you are also a ghost.

An old man blows on the froth of his beer. A young man nods to the song, his white neck gleaming. The hidden truths are agreed-upon, accounted for.

Apostolis laughs to himself across the room. For a moment I feel I'm in on the joke. Then I remember. I haven't crossed the deserts he has crossed.

I am overwhelmed. I love them and want to hold them. Oreana's distance becomes real. The piano waits, untouched. I have given the young girls earrings, a silver mirror as parting gifts. But still I stay.

I descend into the street. The sun descends into Albania. Musicians tune their strings. The thinnest of thumbnail moons undresses above an old shingled roof.

Swallows swirl in the space between rooftops. Orange plaster peels, the wind blows cigarette packets' cellophane wrapping. It all happens at once: the accordions, the sunset, the foot traffic, and my desolation.

The brown eyes of the tourists are like lanterns in priests' hands; the young girls' eyes are like music. Hosts offer their menus desperately. A baby swells in a girl's stomach. She slouches in a cafe chair, scowling. A woman pats her heart, waiting at the cash machine. The music spreads time smoothly between its fingers. I can't leave the town tonight, made crazy by the knocking notes of accordions.

But the town pours me out of its mouth, like a bottle

bored of its contents. Everything hurts, and there is no remedy. Wonder has died and is rotting in my heart.

A boy lays down his plastic gun and pets a yellow dog. The streets become quiet. Inaru, Inaru.

What should it matter if the world is falling apart? Like a wave, it will gather into itself. One day, we will be on the other side of these questions.

The future will happen of its own accord. Which part of this thought-train is me?

I miss places, people. But what does that mean? They do not exist.

Time passes. The island transforms. People become other than what they were. They lose their tragedy, become clouds.

Knowing, hysterical, in the silence.

Athena drives me to the ferry. She lights another slim cigarette and breathes out sharply.

"What?" she says. Her face is different. "I guess I am jealous of you, but in a good way," she says. "You are more free."

She hasn't asked me a question, but I feel like I have to explain. I have taken much. I wonder what I have given. In my center, there is no one—only an idol erected by someone, sentimentally, to watch over a grave.

The sun is setting in the ferry's wake, sinking into Greece. Now it is gone. In the silence of sudden aloneness, many voices rise. My mind drifts, touches each person I know, like dolls left suspended in a paper house.

Dark sea blends into dark sky. The moon lays upon the water a path of living light.

Who am I talking to?

A forest of voices.

A man in a mail truck brings me to the city center—terrifying, clean, orderly, lifeless. The train speaks in a soothing voice, tells us to be careful, to prepare to stop. A strong current of cruelty sweeps the streets clean of homelessness. Along a canal, women sit on stools behind panes of glass, looking at their phones.

"It isn't pretty, sleeping in the park. Not when you're over fifty and you aren't used to it." While he fishes around in his backpack, I glimpse for a moment his toothbrush.

Despair. My heart beating hard. I am water, red and blue. Rain. The church bells intone a melody, minor and off-time.

We don't exist long before our divinity is warped into world. The old struggles have gone away; they don't bother me anymore. The afternoon is frenzied with tourists searching for their hotels. A feeling of cancellation, as if things weren't happening at all.

A woman brings me coffee, a croissant.

"I'm an immigrant too," she says. "We'll take care of you."

Ekim watches me shyly while I am typing beside the canal.

"I'm alone," he says. "Stay with me. As a favor."

He tells me long-buried things: his real name. His ancestry, hidden but unforgotten.

"You are a river," he says. "Watching you is like watching

the water."

The water outside the window, shimmering, chattering and flailing, like someone announcing faraway wars. The water repeats in Ekim's mirrors, in his house of canal and leaves.

Fernando is living in an abandoned museum. His bicycle is covered in barnacles—he pulled it from a canal. He makes soap bubbles in the square for tips—life is difficult on windy days. He shows me photos from his squat in Paris: a father and son on horseback in the mountains. Fernando has thought about them. The father was hard, had suffered. The son was soft, listless. He speaks of Lisboa: the houses, the smells, the poetry.

This morning also blossoms from the old branch. Ekim is giving me the cold shoulder. My mind with its pockets full. Dreams like fingers in soft-boiled eggs. I feel innocent and cloaked.

Splatterings of pain all over the room. Ekim's feet have dry skin, blisters. He has spilled his tobacco on the floor.

Dreams come carrying the truth like fish freshly-snatched from the river. Like silent villagers, the dreams look at me out of dark, mysterious eyes. The fish are still alive, twitching. But they are dying slowly, one by one, at my feet.

A mother touches her son's neck with two fingers wetted in the fountain. Sparrows play between the rooftops. The sound of a radio.

Serena's long brown arms, her scarves whirling, strands of hair stuck to her forehead, cheeks, jaw. Her schoolgirl smile, her basket full of coins.

Maya turned twenty-nine at the stroke of midnight, while she sprayed her finished painting with flame. Judas holds a light in his hand. Or is it something with wings?

The hotel curtains move in the night breeze. Noise below of drunks and prostitutes; the man with the blanket ranting, screeching at passersby.

African men gather under large trees. Typists and tinkerers set up work tables. Europeans in diaphanous dresses sit at cafes. Gypsies pursue them, selling them pieces of their own hunger. I pray atop a hill in a chapel of pink stone whose windows open into quiet worlds. Musicians live in any corner, on any floor of any building. In a tiny room, the memories of Africa gather.

The sky is opaque, ill. Debris in my chest, my face a strange landscape. A drunk man sobs, sitting beside me under the frozen bronze form of a long-gone poet.

"I can't. I'm not made of iron. I can't, I can't. I'm not nothing."

Souls drain through Lisboa. We lose our presence, disappear. Serena in the wind, her cheeks soft and full, deserted by the day, dancing among the empty chairs.

Trying to speak one another's language, we each said goodbye, tongue-tied, like children. Judas stood with the sea at his back while I moved away. I ploughed through the wind into a night dancing blindfolded.

Heartbreak circles, circles, takes a long time to circle

around. We are better than these poor moments. These poor moments that cut through our beauty.

The sky keeps pressing down. How can we lift our heads?

The shadow descends again. Can this really follow that? Underneath the brilliance, the ugliness was always there. We were fools to get carried away.

The little boy who comes every night, open-mouthed, to watch Maya paint—I want to be like that: near to someone's miracles.

They carry God through a street strewn with flowers. God is everywhere, in red drops on the forehead, the earlobes, the palm of the hand. God at the base of the tree, scrawled on the sidewalk. Each doorway is chalked with a different design. Foreheads smeared white: inside, are they awake or sleeping?

One thing after another I throw into the bonfire, but the miracle is already here, with the poised, sun-glossed crows on the dead power line.

Let this wound pour, as the earth is always outpouring, filling the cup of form. Everything hurts—every sound, every sight. Even my thoughts are whips. I am the earth, being tearing through me.

In the temple they fire cannons, but even that boom isn't enough to wake me up.

Old memories hang their heads, their hair dragging sadly below their jaws. All this emptiness is more than I can carry.

Do you like oceans?
oceans are blue
because of the distance
they dress in the hue
of one who is leaving
of one who is vast
of one with no future
one with no past

Do you like oceans?
oceans are you
they wear golden glitter
their skin is so beautiful
but deep down they're heavy
and nobody knows
just how deep down
they go

Do you like oceans?
oceans are true
they told many stories
of mermaids and moons
they buried our clock towers
ate all our jewels
oceans are mothers
and don't suffer fools

5

A chill runs its knuckles over my cheeks. A dose of illness quiets my hopes. I sit here talking to my shadow, while the river passes us by. Moments like ghosts, hand-cuffed together. Humans swarming over a doomed planet.

The island kisses me with rains. Knowing my sore spots, the island pushes on them like hearts she must set beating. Press, press, and take me again to the line I have not crossed, the dawn of the dawn.

Days spent with the teacher. He blows into the harmonium. He strums the guitar. He is a fountain that fills every cup. He even fills my broken cup.

By the light of a metal desk lamp, I page through my old papers, thin as insect wings. Let them curl up in the arms of the tide. One of these days, I will wake up and find I have become the teacher.

Chickens and roosters cross the streets in rows before the sunlight is strong. In the afternoon I sleep, feet above me, on the slant of the roof. In the evening, the ocean heaves. I am back in the world of people I do not understand.

Leaves press like hands in prayer upon the wet pavement—I knock and knock, but no one's there within my soul-house: only wind.

I sit in the lap of the banyan tree. Moaning drifts from the Whistle Bar. Songs with heavy heads, their blossoms too large for their stalks. They nod in the wind and spread their weighty seeds.

All day I walk, swollen, heavy with a strange new sorrow. I have already done this grieving, yet I am doing it again. My words don't come. The evening bears its empty caravan— empty of enchantment.

The softness where their faces move through the air, cheekbones shining. The malice-feathers, slipping out, crimson, from behind the uniform peace. The forest between these bones, where it is still dark. I go in, feel around.

Rumi says to run away from what is comfortable, what is profitable. Gabilan says all he ever wanted was to be a bum.

Harry is living between the parking-lot and the side of the house on a large piece of cardboard. Gabilan has said he's not to be bothered. Harry reminisces about hillbilly music, Dolly Parton's patchwork dress. He is on his way to the water to watch Sparkles the Pig: "You gotta see when he does the pirouette, man. One of these days I'll take you with me. You gotta see it, man, it's the cutest thing."

The moon peeks through the thick, nautical tree. The wind pulls yellow leaves down on the tarp. They make a hissing sound like insects walking. I wake covered in yellow confetti. I find leaves and seaweed in my hair. My combustion carries on. I swim like a dancer, dance against the water. My feet touch the jagged rocks.

The walkers, old-hearted, unconvinced, blue-eyed.

What will we watch now the dancing is done? So much world, hungry to be devoured.

"Only idiots get bored," Gabilan says.

How soft it is: these corpses placid and milky, unperturbed in their clean bowls. I see through the eyes of the people.

They drift in a dangerous, painless state. We will not get away with it, after all.

Absurd music, wild, childlike hilarity in the street, with something metallic at the bottom. The knifelike despair of my face changing, like a beach fluttering and wrinkling through the tides. I braid my hair.

I can't reason with the monster in me, but I can be near it.

They say the night will be cold. All is well. I walk through the graveyard with eyes closed. A sore mercy in me and in everyone.

Gabilan says, "Why don't you get a hobby like fixing bikes? Do something useful for a change." They have cared for me like a family, given me rest, love, space.

Ecstatic evening, unraveling, loose and lapping inside. Simon, painting alone in the abandoned street.

There is no more of me to pare, to split into slivers. I have become my atoms, I have ceased to exist. A moment ago, it hurt. Now, there is nothing to hurt.

My heart ran clear and loving beneath the juicy twisting trees. The smell of night flowers. Strange, clawing thoughts.

Pieces of light on the street. All the things left lying around in the mind, awake with chatter. The pieces of light slip up the walls. A bell is ringing, although it isn't heard.

My heart has almost disappeared. It is a tiny wispy thing that I must swaddle and feed, a pin-point of light swimming in an endless field. Someone has turned me off, luckily, and I go on colliding with things like a marionette.

I have died inside myself. By touch I feel in the dark. Fear dresses in plans. I feel the drifty depression, dancing like seaweed in the tide. My light is soft and refracted. My soul comes and sits down in my body.

I look in the mirror. I see myself pitifully. How badly I want to be with the people, to burn up with them in evening's empire. How unsure I am of their acceptance. I worry, for the world regains its richness. When this happens, it is not fair—it is unpaid-for, and it will be taken away.

What has happened here? Have I been dreaming for months? My flesh hanging on me as if it expects something to come and help it along. Words and money keep me from union. I look at the sea without seeing. The dust of attachment. I become citified, propped up by toothpicks. I suspect that everything I have thought has been wrong.

Inaru knows—he points to the very place. How could anyone do thus by trying?

I call to my soul on the pier. She sits with her back turned, tearing something up in her hand. I do automatically. I wait for the turbidity to clear. Plans form, growing legs in the darkness. I write around the truth. Most of me has gone to another place. I carry on, pull the two-legged body through the cycle of actions. Money organizes the hours, not wonder. That is what the soul means to say with her silence.

A treatment coming to me like an animal on a table.

I look up into the tree.

The human movers are clumsy. I love them on the long roads. They seem far away. A strange new wanting is born. The truths sprawl much wider than words. Things misbehave. The island of impatient toys. The beauty always bled off the page.

I look in the mirror. I remember a past riddled with suffering, but the source of the suffering is gone.

The sludge of cosmic change, the material dragging behind the spirit. The urge to atone. The desire to help, to make things right. Cloudedness, inefficiency.

Who has hurt you today, that you run in the fields attacking reeds?

Our words cover the gaping hollow, but they are poor bridges, made of poor materials: gossip, politics, anything but the truth.

We meet as oil and water, sliding over one another without touching, all our ions fleeing. Eyes averted, sadness flourishing in our faces, though we try to smile.

We eat yucca, potatoes, okra, rice, coconut meat. I sit on the bench while Inaru talks about the price of apple juice.

"How much?" he demands. "You're from the USA. You must know how much a gallon of apple juice costs."

His failure becomes my failure. I feel the heart wilting and greying in my chest. There is not enough love here.

The soul alone with its thoughts—the one-way roads of my sentences drop away. I am only this pain, this vertigo.

I wake with the trees. The freeze still clings to me, an anguish I treat gently, hold patiently. I hear drums, unidentifiable losses. My love pours out, indiscriminate. I fall into the arms of the future. I am big. My eyes are burning. The heaviness of old men on their poor ankles, the ticking desperation of their misery, a love with no source, no handles.

The sadness is with me now that has been with me in each new city, in each new solitude. But the sadness is merely my body, my vehicle. I must learn to stand outside of my draped windows and carry on—there are gifts in here that must be delivered, bang to the heart where they are needed.

Roads of longing wind out like open hands reaching for unknown souls. There is no mercy, yet there is. The tragedy of womanhood—the utter loss. The power latent and imprisoned and hopeless.

Suddenly, I believe again. The heart does not make mistakes. He will do the thing, illuminated like a candle someone lit and set to float down the river. He doesn't speak my language. He speaks poetry. He sees from above. He goes the long way. I see what he means. I get ready to help.

The sadness of a door closing. The street swept clean. Friday afternoon comes along to pollute it. A wall of wanting rises up, keeping me from the moment I am in. Nice faces pass by. I keep looking over my shoulder.

The night is full of adoration. Undulation of the panic. The walkers have no fear—my dreams headless, dancing without their heads.

The fears are here—the corners not turned, the heavy chain of moments, dark rivers of eyes. Fearful awakeness, empty-handed night.

I feel as if I'd never met Inaru, as if he had just appeared in the seams of the blue street. A proud man, a man holding keys, free of that iridescent fog, freshly-cut from the earth, straight up and down as he must once have stood. I let the shadow-puppet fall. I take my scissors to my harp strings and cut them one by one.

Desperation in the midnight sun. I take my moment off. Look at my mask at the bottom of the glass. Skeletons in sequined dresses. The chaos of the street doesn't give me the chance to suffer like a scarecrow in the place of passersby.

Tourists in pastel clothing drift over the island like weather. I find love for the objects around me—a dress, swinging from the tent pole. Cloth bags, the Spanish dictionary. The blue skirt I am using as a towel.

The same songs nightly spill from the Whistle. Duval Street, your trees are turning blue and I am slipping from your gentle branch. A unicyclist is practicing in the parking-lot. The baby goes on changing. Here is the love, my finger is on it.

Pain bristles and skates through the street. A woman sits on the concrete, coughing, and asks walkers for money.

Harry returns from the hospital with new clothes. He talks about the American "ice dancers" in the Olympics.

"They have culture," he says. "The other ice dancers just start skating at a million miles an hour right when the music starts. These two know how to go with the music."

He blinks and smiles through his beard.

Samantha comes, her face thick with makeup, in a tight dress.

"I was trying to make peace with the universe," she says. She pauses, lights a cigarette, writes the rest of the sentence on a piece of paper.

The smell of coconut oil, the beaded curtain rattling. Biking home in the soft night. The street is still awake. I read on the rooftop. The neat smoothness of some moments. Our lucid stupidity, clumsiness, sailing through the lit-up world. Something splits me open from the inside. My soul is a dripping jungle. I have just emerged and am waiting at a traffic light. Every city is foreign. My soul came from the fisher-birds. Can I build my love here, on the empty street?

Joy so suddenly turns to terror. A coin flipping in the air. The theater of the day begins. I am unable to see from all angles. I exist, spooked, like something in a dream.

I see Harry with his walker. I hurry past him. I can't stop to listen to his complaints.

"Those kids are evil, man!" he calls after me.

"Were they chasing the chickens?"

"Yeah, torturing the little babies. Pure evil!"

I wake today with this desperate seed—I should be doing something.

"That's fine," Gabilan says, "if you have somewhere to go. But we're going to the grave."

More are coming. I see them growing in the women. We each carry our share of the terrible weight.

The clouds return me to moments that are buried. The wind chimes are speaking about a friend they have lost.

Under a full moon, Ana and I drink a tiny bottle of Fireball. We sit on the broken bench. Bottles accumulate on the table—bottles of compliance. I tell stories, but I cannot be found in my voice or in my words. My feet don't seem to be connected to my mouth.

Ana is paralyzed by pain. The moon disapproves of our choice of poisons. Why these green bottles, all dressed up like soldiers? I sketch Ana's eyes while she talks. We pile the weight higher and higher. We bury ourselves.

A rooster crowed. I shivered. The sky was still dark. In the grey dawn, the rain soaked me. Now and then I got up and emptied the tent pockets of water. I nestled back into the wet blankets, tied the skirt around my eyes, and slept.

The trees remember an older America. The air is luxuriant, spacious, as if outside of existence. The people glide like boats. They make mistakes as if they had forever.

All morning in ecstasy on the roof. I lie head-down on the slant, my pulse running through me like children in a soft landscape. I put my black skirt over my face. The island fills up with sufferers. I can't control the beauty. It burns higher and higher.

New shades of howlings, new howlings in me. There are no choices. They rolled off the rooftops. Endeavors fall away. I am a light.

Tragedies all over your face. In the darkness of my blindfold, I remembered things that seem astonishing now.

The chandelier in the theater. The theater of the mind. He never saw how I was delivering God in little rivulets from heaven to the earth, just as he was.

I watched him watch the trees.

A man was singing on the sand. These Caribbean clouds are my sisters.

I can't get any older. I'm as old as I could get.

Inaru kisses me on the cheekbone. He plays the guitar covered in fire-dust. His expression is chaotic.

Wellness on the face of the passing woman. She has prepared her clothing, her mouth and her skin; she moves through the afternoon like a seaworthy ship. I wake up in this moment, the world spreading before my eyes.

"I'm the black sheep of the family," the man with the parrot is saying. The wife is smiling graciously while her husband is trying to get away. The afternoon is drifting slowly over the sidewalk. Husbands in the shadows of their wives.

This week will blow away like the bad smell that for days wreathed the island. They said it was the sugarcane burning in Cuba.

My shadow wants to touch the road. My mind blisters with poems, symbols, crackling truths.

The slow giving-way—I can only see what has changed by looking at what has not changed. This pain like footprints across my face.

I am good and desperate again, hollow as a singing bowl. I have thrown all my stones, but none skipped. I am pinned like a specimen to the island. Time burns through; my wings make crazy colors.

I feel time falling out of me like an afterbirth. America, with her eyes lit. Heads of women float vapidly above their pastel dresses. Vendors are closing their stands in the dusk. Having lost something nameless, I go on. I clean up my chaos, organize my nightmares. I pass through a doorway to another world.

They were puppets and mirrors. Beauty and silence, my soul rolling around in my life, knocking into things, rubbing up against them. Things change. The way they have been gives way to another way.

They are not finished yet, my people. It is a blue evening. The sadness is uniform. Everywhere I go, it is the same.

Inaru is at the pier. I can see that he is happy even from a distance, with his back turned. There are children near him, he is handing one of them something. The sky is overcast. There won't be a sunset.

A mystery pressing its nose close to our glass. I put the foam mattresses in the dryer. I shake the leaves from my hair. I bind new books. Plant debris carpets the yard. The ladder is speckled with paint and footprints. The island breathes on my cheeks in the morning. The ecstasy of the rooftop world.

Look at this tub of wine, I kept saying. The noises poisonous. Mortality all over us. In the arms of Higgs Beach.

"Coral dust," Cage says.

"The whole world is evil," the violinist says. "The only thing that is not evil is the thing that does not exist."

Graveyard dreams. The Green Parrot, with its colloquial nightmare, its lurid intimacy.

"You do not give me joy, but I am often joyful near you."

I play the guitar atop the yellow canoe.

"Poets aren't supposed to have money," Gabilan says. "They're just supposed to have sorrows."

I went out into the world like a master, but I only fought the clothes hanging in the closet. I ran from the simplest of truths, but the simplest of truths caught up with me.

My angel shows up around noon. He puts his mouth to my arm. Giving or taking—it isn't certain.

The island patters with feet. So many of my eyes already covered over, patted firm in the dirt.

The trials come. Walls harden. There is less space for miracle. Laws fall around like sunlight.

The wind knocks down the box fan. I prop it up with Shakespeare's Works Volume II and a conch.

I'm asking again: why is it so? Poems spread out like feathers. I descend into the sordid. It has all been written: the glitter and the fever. A skeleton rides past me on his bicycle. A lost soul sits with his hands on his knees, contemplating his next bold move, a feather in his hat.

Peace returns from her mission in the hills. Days pass like a procession. I sit until I remember the language of colors and waves. I sit in a pool of myself, blue and pink and humming.

I pick my own cherries from the branches now.

Ning sent me a painting of a woman that looked like me, a letter that says, "Every soul suffers a lot, and has its own path."

He adds a quote from The Little Prince. "If you say you'll come at four o'clock, my heart will begin to be happy."

These hands came from the others. There is no one to defend you from yourself. Today I am human. I can only think of love. The blue is blue in the sky so blue. Heavy cords of earthliness. I walk along the shadows. Promises are hidden in crumbling courtyards, regrets fall heavily in the hot sunlight. The clouds are eloquent, take a deep bow. The city is talking in its sleep—it doesn't want to wake up. Good, kind faces.

Bare necks in the jewelry store window—headless, bodiless necks, bare of gems for the night.

I dreamed there was an empire, that its tanks and missiles lay on the beaches. I dreamed of helicopters and jets in the sky.

Dreamy, dreary saxophone notes in the galleries of a vacant downtown. There is no one to tell. I walked with the flowers and the stars and the moon. I walked with the palms and the porches and the lights.

I'm the only one who can see the setting sun, this dream born a captive, born condemned.

My face cries. Tears strike over my face. Yet stillness inside, the words, "All is well." Something is broken, but not me. I have grown tall.

The island has become a place in my heart. It has all the marks of a place.

"When will you stop moving?" a voice asks.

"When will you stop lingering?" asks another voice.

The world with its apparitions, drawn thinly over the thrashing dream.

I wish Jesus was here
to explain the wet miracles
to let me know nothing has changed

I'm God too, so they say
but my wings, what a weight
and the years wrote my story so strange

But I guess I'm protected
by the heart in my chest
I never meant anybody any harm

I was born in the empire
and I rendered unto Caesar
every bangle that jingled on my arm

But if he were here then at least I would know
I didn't miss anything not being born long ago
and I'd sleep a little easier
knowing no one's dreaming better
and the curtains are still closed at the shows

6

The heaviness departed with its caravan, having told here enough stories, having smoked its long pipes to ash.

The water speaks to me. The hills speak to me. Kentucky with its craggy curses. The water, full of eternity. The Southern evil.

The conversation's glassy surface, while in my mind the charnel ground smolders.

Mist in the valleys. Worlds overlapping. Jets undressing the silence of the skies.

My soul has curled into a little fist, worried about the future.

Gabilan says the future will be like the past. I can't believe it.

Do I want the sea, or am I the sea?
Lightning bugs in the trees. Wind in the trees.

Paul: "I am no longer in a state of emergency. I'm grieving. I'm almost done."

Every day, he cries, his daily chore.

A family of geese on the shore of the lake. There are nine of them. They wade into the water, drift away.

I pull aside the curtain. There are the sorrows, the pains, like dolls, like idols on an altar. One sorrow, a purple tongue, rising out of my lap, through my trunk, curling like a python around my head.

Judas said, "Go home. It's time to go home." Judas, tap-dancing on the slick Lisboa tiles.

Paul said goodbye as if he was saying hello—with a greeting in his eyes.

"You need to be loved," said the boat captain. "Loved, loved, loved."

Winds breathe over the trees. Winds breathe over me. But I am not a tree. Is this my whistling sound?

The water says, "love me."
The water is love.

I'm terrified by America, where the miracle is always turning off.

The orphaned white beach in Pondicherry, the sea-grape trees growing at intervals, the plastic bags doing somersaults. Vagrant children and fat tourists, chai booths and fruit-sellers with secrets in their eyes.

The water rippling, flowing, moving with the wind. The wind patters the leaves. Crickets talk, frogs chant. Green, unreal green all around.

My body seems far away, like a country I am wandering through.

I look at the house beside the lake. It is solid, made of brick. But I can see right through it.

Build up a house, build up a story. Everything is always vanishing.

If you sit still enough you can hear the past and future.

No one can hear me, complains my heart.

But I hear.

The distant beauty, which I can feel even from here.

You can't go out looking for the beauty. It's always traveling, like the rain. I can hear it coming—it will be here any moment.

The desire to be happy.

Two currents flow through one another, shimmering.

Reading my formless soul like a map in a lost language. What does it say? I have been reading it wrong.

I hear my music now: somber, deep, free, and unfixed. She is here now, my soul, so long coming.

She closes her ears to the guessing and gambling, the flailing about.

Confusion will return, but not yet.

I've been putting importance on the things that are unimportant.

The evening coming with something in its mouth.

Dizzy, tired, hopeless, nothing coming out of me—no fruit on the tree.

It angered me. Now I live with it, like a corpse I'm carrying around.

This taste runs like a river through my memories: the hope that I might devise a way out.

Perhaps I have not become sorrowful enough. Maybe the only way out is through total despair. To welcome the pain, the obsession, the ugliness. To pile them on until the sufferer is destroyed.

Breath roaring through the trees. Sadness, panic. The geese see me coming, launch flapping into the lake. Wind stirs the water. Far away, a train whistle blows.

Echoes of the island push into my consciousness. The sparrows are frantic, furious with my presence.

I didn't choose to be alone. There was simply no one on my path.

Wind around me, sun on skin. Feelings of loss, emptiness.

Prying urgently through the woods. An unanswered chaos.

The grass is full of dragonflies.

The unreal, shimmering day. The world too bright, my soul hiding in darkness.
On the hill, bliss, ecstasy in the grass. I find myself dancing in the wind, stalking the forest, cooing like a wounded bird.

Losses drumming through the mind. Nothing matters. It's all contained; the river doesn't need help flowing.

Heavy, sleepy, disconsolate. I'm becoming an old woman, though I still have dreams in which I'm young. Trying to untie the threads on this cloudy day, trying to remember what came before ignorance and limitation.

I grow tired and blue. Cursed hope keeps getting aroused. I work up a vision of myself, then realize most of me is missing. Too much stupidity residing in this perspective. This perspective that has been hatched from an egg.

When will you stop objectifying yourself? Chasing thoughts around like a police man. Why don't you leave those thoughts alone?

The lake in the rain, a raven in a moss-covered tree.

Sitting on a fallen tree across shallow water. Our value is inherent, not in manifested things. Pale green algae over the water, trembling pieces of sky. The lake carries white sky on its many backs. Acceptance is dawning.

The same inner world, wherever I go in the outer world. Nothing to bring back to the people—things are not needed. I am invincible—the miracle has already been achieved. Each path rolling out from me with its little grail at the end. But I am a grail. I am a grail already.

No one is going to take me by the hand and show me who I'm supposed to be. I have to take myself by the hand. "I'm not lost," says my mind, looking at the lake.

Visions on the outside—leaves, material. On the inside, only soul. The soul of everything is my soul. So many doors inward. Suffering is one door. "They gaze coolly on my door of suffering."

An ocean in me. Things near the surface seem distant, small. Beside the lake I hear the murmurs of an earlier self. It's meaningless: the projects, the literature, the teaching, the steel trap.

"A steel trap can't hold the ocean."

What kind of face does an ocean wear?
An ocean can only love the face of death.

An old frequency is taking my hand these dark and cloudy days, the same sounds I couldn't abide the first time.

I smell my child self in the sunburnt hills, the manure and pollen blowing off the sea of limestone.

The Kentucky sea, grown earthy, where I first learned loneliness.

Gabilan: "Face your demons. What are you running from?"

Trying to become the world—empty and rustling, shimmering like the lake, allowing, quiet. Learning to say "Ah."

The echoes of my life seem meager. I fly out another way. A second passageway, through form. Such a struggle—all happening in a dream!

Poetry is only form. Nothing, just form.

What's wrong with me? Trying to open my muscles, untie the cords of bondage—human being is a condition, an ailment. I've heard it before. Now I feel it.

Roughness in my soul. I am tattered, grotesque. I try to smooth it over, but there is no gloss that can fill in the deformity. Could it be that somewhere deep I have always merely been searching for my way to pray?

I begin to have dreams and visions. There is a taste in things, intoxicating richness. Time is a caress. I am in a gift.

May I also be a gift. May my body contain gifts. There is enough of everything, and "all are welcome."

A body like a clean river, existing to nourish.

A whippoorwill is singing near the old lake. Engines in the sky. I come back from the underworld where I have traveled for two days. We are all, each, divine, on a divine course.

I have been through such forests. Forests where words are needless and unthinkable, where song is superfluous, where arms and legs seem like the long way of getting there.

My soul is dark, full of soot. The night is full of soot.

Thoughts fuse together in primal darkness, female and sorrowful. I am a sorrowful thing in the lap of the conditionless.

I have one tin coin to slip into the hand of the world. But I can't find it. I'm swimming in coins.

My stars fell out of the sky, into the sea.

In the forest, I don't feel like a poet, I feel like water. Currents of pain.

There is nothing to say, no method for saying it, no one to say it to. The pain with its ferris wheels, its circus rings.

The leaves in the wind sound like bells to my ears. Again, the world is filled with bells.

The shadow of the hawk while it is circling. Mind thick, stirred-up, full of dust.

"Out of the unconditional space rose the unconditional question: what?"

Heaviness: as if my flesh were made of ghosts, the ghosts of dead moments.

After groping in the intangible mind, the world of form seems exquisite: the bathroom floor, the lamp-switch, the sketchbook.

Blue night, face hidden. Lake sounds, moon hidden. One star. I pace under the porch, a new gift in my mind. I didn't always have ears. There are other ways of hearing.

Sock-feet roll into the concrete. I am stepping!

I have another body besides this body, my body of ripples, of closets and coins. Thick cloud completely covering the farm. I am part of the farm-body, warmed by the blanket of cloud. This thing in me, this tongue of awareness, feeling, sentience. It is not only me, it is the farm, the crickets, the birds, the people.

It is also the places that are not the farm. All the beings that have touched it, contributed to it, merged with it.

The lake is also it, strains the same world through its own manner of sieve—we are the same thing, filtered differently.

How lonely I have sometimes been for myself, in this attic filled with lockets. When I move, I leave behind my body and soul.

Let me not think of leaving now. I hear a plane rumbling above the clouds—above the blanket of clouds that warms the farm.

The emotions are foolish armies, rising in defense of some hidden queen. They go flocking over mountain ranges, can't be called back easily.

The dead trees like bones yellowed by the light. The sun is kissing the horizon goodnight. Birds play among the dead trees that rise out of the lake like amputees.

Fish move, spreading rings. Ravens caw, jets rumble. I can still look at God, though I have a whole circus in my eye.

The sun is in the pines. The shadows are wearing eye patches.

I am not better than I was; I am not better than I will be. I have always been the same, and I will never change. No time has passed. All time hangs in a bouquet of colors, clinging to a center: is.

Hawks in the sky, over the road. The curling stamen in a

purple flower. The veins in the leaves. The wide leaves like saucers, blue at an angle. There are no blank spaces. The mind is also covered—covered in suchness.

I read the Heart Sutra, the Sermon on the Mount, Jesus's parables. I sit watching the lake a long time and pray: "May imperfect form awaken to perfect wisdom. May the shadow be resolved in love."

The sky and lake are blue, the trees and grass are dark. In the morning I think about my skeleton.

I can see what I am doing—my programs, the things I want.

Let go, I tell myself. I've never been able to completely let go. And so it's always been my choice—to stay attached.

Difficulty concentrating. Chains of thoughts. I trace them back to absurd triggers.

The lake is turquoise and blushing silver in the morning.

An image in the Upanishads: two birds on the branch. One is the small self, the other is God. When the small self eats the fruit, God watches, not eating. Fruits of karma, of history and form.

When I eat there is also the part of me that does not eat: that is God. It is for this that people fast. So that the small self can grow fainter, and God can be revealed.

This is the end of every path—dissolution.

Nothing abides, except for flux—the flux that is emptiness of abiding. The receiver is a gesture, like the giver.

The lake is no-color, and thus it is many-colored—brown of mud, blue of distance, white of cloud carrying water over the hills. Green of life, of sun-drinking leaves.

Olive is coming today, any minute. I find I live toward her, preparing something for her.

I feel I am abandoning the place and all its members— the hawks, the trees, the lakes. I shed tears at the top of the hill beside the old lake, the place that feels most sacred. I walk like a dreamer, by hazard.

The waning moon was high and bright, the lake still and reflecting the bright-edged clouds. I watched the moon's reflection dancing and splitting like a candle's flame.

Fog moved between the lake and the sky. Everything is mind. The fears are mind, too. Until I embrace them, there will be no freedom. I cannot escape the worn paths if I'm still afraid of the wolves in the woods.

Symmetrical patterns in the Queen Anne's Lace and in the clover. The mind as mandala, and our journey through life toward death a journey through a mandala.

An insect in the tiny curling stamen of the flower. Such love, such tenderness there. Elegance in the veins of the leaves, the same design everywhere you look. The wind rustles in the treetops.

Poses of death still disturb and frighten me. I suppose I will have to go through them to understand. One has to go through everything.

Underneath my small thoughts, the coarse distractions, my soul is like a person with her ear to a door—listening, anticipating. Is it the ego, listening for itself to be vindicated, made real? Tension, blockage.

Suzuki: there is no division, in or out. One world on both sides of the door.

Even in the rich and meaningful life, the wasteland is there, as a layer, under everything, inside of it. Even in moments of enchantment, the knowledge that things will end, that everything doesn't fill the emptiness.

Was there a time before duality, a time when there was nothing?

The hill is covered with Queen Anne's Lace. The lake is like a jewel or a lady in a dress.

Olive brought a bottle of whiskey, wrapped up in a tapestry. We drank on the dock. The piercing moon lit the whole sky. The water waved all around us.

Olive talked about bombs and war. And yet the lake is quiet. What does the lake know, under her glittering surface?

The hues of blue in the morning, the hues of red in the afternoon. God in the grass: a housefly cleaning itself on a blade of grass.

I watch the moon in the water, shaking, and the moon in the sky, still. The same thing that makes it still makes it shake.

I watch the moon being born out of the treetops, yellow-red.

The night sounds: warbling, snarling, splashing, a howl. What looks like a log swims toward me on the dock. I get up and it turns around, swims off the other way.

Olive joins me on the dock. She sees another shooting star.

My eyes are veiled
this Ohio town
with its rusted rails
with its clouded hours
with its stars burnt out
with its matches wet
with its volume down
on its TV set

All the semaphores
know their lines by heart
and they slip right through
the golden part
and the sun declines
and the traffic flows
and the neon advertisements glow

And the present's all
tied up in bows
I see heaven as long
as my eyes are closed

My bags are packed
but they weigh me down
and they jingle jangle
full of fallen towers
full of graveyard flowers
with plastic stems
full of deities
too stiff to bend

And the moments fall
and the hourglass weeps
for her mouth is small
but her hunger's deep

and our minds still dance
though they have no feet
in their cabaret
full of empty seats

While the preacher casts
to swine his pearls
I'm in the world at last
the famous world

Now my heart's so clean
you can see right through
and the inmates freed
and the caged birds too
and the ladies shine
like marionettes
and their brows incline
and their paint is wet
and the men of fog
equivocate
they sing the song
of rusted gates

The men of God
just evaporate
their boats are gone
and so's their wake
they brought no copper
wore no shoes
they burned so hot
their fire was blue

And all that's left
in this Ohio town
is your shadow
and some leaves of brown

7

A host of worries and plans flocks around me. I return to the things themselves—they are harmless, gentle things. I open the decrepit Bible, read about Jesus examining the coin, saying, "Whose face is this? Then give these things to him."

I sit in the darkened room. A car drifts down the street. The air conditioner hums, the sounds of the safe and dreamy suburb. How very human I am, how unlike my heroes, my Seymours, my Jesuses, my angels and saints in their glitter and paint. How petty, how feeble I am.

This morning, Mom made eggs and toast with butter and gave me the last of Aunt Darlene's peach preserves. The space and gentleness that allow such things to happen. What kind of beast could ask for more?

The sounds of crickets, the sound of a sister's voice saying, "I'm not going to bed this minute." The tall, tall trees, a town singing with trains and roads. The sky purple and bright, the miracle with me, close at hand.

Time means we don't exist. Listen to the crickets, listen to your hunger. Thoughts go off like fireworks, some hang there burning in the sky, some leave trails of smoke.

Heaviness, city air. People look sick—women in their makeup, the wrinkles of longtime smokers. Bulkiness. Jackal souls.

The sky is grey and marbled like a tombstone.

Placelessness, abjection. The man with the sack of flour, dreaming of how he will spend the money it will fetch, who dies, mid-daydream, when the sack falls from the rafters and lands on his head.

I woke from panicked dreams and achy sleep. I went to the ravine penitent and ailing.

The frailty of the human self. There isn't much of me to sacrifice. I will go quickly into the pile of matchsticks.

The street preacher explains to me that Santa Claus is really Satan.

"God doesn't want people to keep saying the same thing to him over and over. He wants to be spoken to like a friend."

Olive says God's not conscious, not listening to us, not making decisions.

"But is God unconscious? Like a jellyfish?" I ask.

"What are you trying to say about jellyfish?"

"God would have to be omniscient," I say. "God would not only know what we were thinking, it would be us—all of us, feeling and experiencing us thoroughly."

Olive spends hours cooking rice and beans. I brought groceries. It seems like a miracle, yet it is not a miracle. It is only possible through deprivation elsewhere, which gives the action a sinfulness.

The space around me, the gentleness of time, the harmlessness of the stream, the predictable mode of the rocks. Are these conditions created by unseen altruism, the efforts of monks and hermits, beings in other dimensions?

Olive finishes the beans, only to discover that the rice

cooker has never been on. She plays the accordion while we wait. We are practicing the Jacques Brel song, "L'eclusier." Olive feeds Febe some of her beans, dropping spoonfuls in the porch: splat, splat.

We walk in the ravine. I fall behind, take off my shoes, look into the water.

I am thirsty, but I dare not drink this water. Things might be different if I dared. I might dare if things were different. Things might be different if things were different.

In the gospel of Mary, Jesus says, "There is no sin. You make sin."

Could it be that love and hate need one another, have something in common? That the very thing they have in common is divinity?

My feet are in the water, feeling the water. Somehow, this is surprising, miraculous. On some level, my mind is looking for the "right" way to be.

Olive is happy, talking about the fallen tree, walking ahead. She is sure.

Poems come sometimes, but I let them go. We walk in the water. I see Olive standing there. How can it be that someone so important is so small? I look at the rock—its old, graceful way. Oldness in me, too.

Olive looks for poke-berries. We wake up from naps and she dresses me for work. She ties Grandma's yellow flower bracelet onto my wrist.

I hear crickets and engines. The garbage disposal is

broken; water is standing in the sink. Dishes pile up. Keys are lost, phones are broken, food is rotting, forgotten about in the refrigerator. No one knows why the dog is losing such quantities of hair.

I try to build hope. Whatever you build, dear one, must fall.

A tiny spirit in the left, lower corner—the God I have ignored. You cannot serve two masters; attachment to physical, small-self concerns eclipses this aspect.

The mother in the being, the familiarity of the physical form—smooth carpets of blood, the old relics in the mind— the ballet shoes, the bric-a-brac, the bowl of grapes on the kitchen counter. Music boxes and clocks that count the hours.

The father comes, flashes of proverbs from a deep center of the mind.

"If anyone offers you heaven, refuse it, but give them whatever payment they ask."

Poems come to me in my sleep, but the waking mind loses them. I feel my cheekbones with my fingers: it is not here.

The street becomes a poem. I begin to suspect that all ordinary life bears a mark of blasphemy. But Zooey says, "Be God's actress."

Uncle Ben: We are the glory of God. What kind of God? What kind of glory?

"Examine your intention," the teacher says. "If you can't share a meal with someone, you've got a problem. On the bodhisattva path, you will be called upon to give your life."

To clear oneself as sacred ground. What else is there?

I pass through dazzling towns. Huge trees, enigmatic scenes, fields of high corn.

My face frightens me in the mirror. I fear it will betray me somehow. Betray what? I feel that I am guilty, that people can tell by looking.

The first line of song I can distinguish goes directly to my soul: "How long will you love what is futile and seek what is false?"

Another line drifts up out of history, fluttering on the soft voices of the monks. It is an answer to a question which I have carried here with me: "Darkness and light are both alike to thee."

I pursued and overtook my foes,
never turning back till they were slain.
I smote them so they could not rise;
they fell beneath my feet...

They cried, but there was no one to save them;
they cried to the Lord, but in vain.
I crushed them fine as dust before the wind;
trod them down like dirt in the streets.

I squirm at the familiar violence, aggression. At the back of the chapel, a plaque of Mary is bathed in golden light. They sing to her: we are crying children in a terrible world of suffering, but you are our merciful mother.

The prajnaparamita, the mother who said the fateful

words, "Let it be." Let it be: the suffering, and the rest of it as well. Was that merciful?

Uncle Ben's voice over the phone is like Grandma's.

"We go to bed at seven," he says with a chuckle. He speaks like someone who has long lived among foreigners.

I walk around a small lake surrounded by willows and pines. A purple blush falls over the fields. The red brick and neatly mown lawn return me to that sturdy, landscaped world. I ponder the words of Jesus, "Blessed are the poor in spirit, for theirs is the kingdom of heaven." My thoughts are tangled, bound around a simple question: what am I?

Memories echo strangely. I sit under a willow, before a statue of Mary. Let the past then be no more than an echo, a ripple, a color in the sky.

It occurs to me that perhaps they were not singing about emerging unscathed from battle, but about that which is indestructible, that which destruction itself cannot destroy.

A square of quilt in the bathroom: a pattern of shapes whose points meet at the center. The center is the absence of shape, the dance of form that surrounds the formless mind. The sensation again of pure awareness.

Trivia, moments, scraps of dream. But they are only imprints, drawings in the sands of the mind. "Knowledge is the fire that obliterates all form." Can knowledge be an ocean wave that washes away the vestiges of futile moments, the meanness of children who have long since grown up?

I still fear my shadow, still worry, "What will they think?"

The heavy door of the abbey opens slowly. A tiny old man emerges, bright-eyed, leaning on a cane. His long white robe is drawn at the waist by a belt. His charcoal hair is cut close, his white beard has been left a while to grow. His eyes are black, generous, his cheekbones high, his nose high-bridged, pointing down like an arrow from his elegantly flared nostrils.

"It's nice to see you after all these years," he says in a wavering voice. He shakes my hand. I ask how long it has been.

"I think you were about this high," he says, holding his hand, palm down, to his waist. But I was older than that.

"I can remember when your mother was a toddler. I turned 88 a few days ago. I don't feel it, but I know better." He looks at me brightly. "Would you like to take a walk?"

We walk toward the sunrise. He speaks of my great-grandfather, the mayor. He was an orphan when he came to America after the potato famine. He rose up through the railroad union; he used to read Shakespeare to his children at night after drinking at the bar.

"Isn't that something? Where do you suppose this Irish orphan developed a taste for Shakespeare?"

At Latin school Ben learned several languages. He enlisted at 17 and worked in a Navy hospital. After the war, he finished medical school. There, he became interested in philosophy and had long phone conversations with his sweetheart.

"She was a violinist. When she played, there was more feeling, more eloquence, than in the performances of professionals. I gave her the ring on the day I graduated. I went on to be a medical resident, and she stayed at school, but we kept in close touch.

"In those days, I was waking up early every morning and attending mass before doing rounds. I was working in close contact with trauma and death. I reflected that, well, life is short. And if I really loved her, I should encourage her to focus on the next life. And if she did so, I should, too.

"You see, she was a Southerner, and the daughter of a wealthy lawyer. She was used to being well off and had all the benefits of that world. I told her my decision, and she reacted as I knew she would. She said, 'Are you sure?' And I said, 'Yes, I'm sure.' And that was what we did."

"Did she—become a nun?"

"She's still a nun to this day. She was the superior of her order, and I was the abbot here, as you know. She was a very good teacher, became the principal of the school, and so forth."

"I've—never heard a story like that."

"No," Ben agrees thoughtfully. "It's unusual."

We sit on a bench before a lake. In the lake there are three islands. From the shore to the first island, there is a small foot bridge.

"There was a stream here," Ben says, "running down to the river. I thought we should dam it up. You know, to have a lake near a monastery—it's meditative and so on. Anyway, that was agreed upon. I was reading a book at the time which stated that at the first level of spiritual development, you can make progress through your own will—and the grace of God, of course. At that level you are dealing with your disordered emotions, your bad habits, and so-forth. At the next level, the level of the soul, you can no longer proceed by your own efforts, but you must be carried by faith. The third island represents the level of the spirit. To reach this island, you must be carried by faith and divine assistance."

He presses his thumb into the hollow of his cheek.

"What is the difference between soul and spirit?"

"Good question! I can tell you're a Westerner. Soul in Greek is psyche: mental components. Spirit, on the other hand, is breath, wind. This is the God level."

He doesn't mention the Tibetan word for mind: sems, the heart-mind, the home of song.

"There are as many connections in the human mind as there are stars in the sky," Ben says. "Plato says this universe is just a shadow. It doesn't look like it, but when you examine what things are, below the surface, you find a lot of information."

"Do you believe there is an objective reality?"

"I have no doubt about it. But there is also an unseen world. It says so in the Apostles' Creed. Do you remember? 'I believe in God, the father almighty, creator of heaven and earth. Of all that is visible and invisible...'"

Our talk is like fingers shaping the darkness. I ask an old question of mine: "After all, what is energy?"

"In Genesis," Ben says mischievously, "it says something very interesting. Do you want to hear it in Hebrew?" He recites the verses in Hebrew, then in English: "God created heaven and earth, but it was all mixed up, all confused. Then, he said, 'Let there be light.' And it's true that before the Big Bang, when everything was so densely packed together in the singularity, stars could not form. They formed later, as everything began to spread out."

"Was there a time before the singularity?"

"Some of these things are beyond our understanding."

"Buddhists say we are all potentially omniscient," I suggest. "That we can know everything intuitively, if we are realized—"

"Not omniscient. We can expand our horizons exponentially. But only God is infinite."

I look at the horizon stretching out around us. The cornfields fade gradually into the distance, without disappearing for a long time. I remember how large the world is.

A truck rumbles down the lane. Ben waves.

"That's Sam. He was a Marine. The armed forces are like a family, you know. He's come to pick up the bread. That truck can hold 30,000 loaves. We make about 15,000 a day. When I was in charge of production, it was 18,000. That was the regular thing.

"There is only so much you can know empirically. The rest depends on faith. That's why it baffles me that so many scientists these days claim to be atheists."

"What do you mean by faith?"

"Faith means intuition based on evidence. We act on faith all the time. You drove here. You made about a thousand acts of faith on the way. Our personal relationships, the way the world functions day to day. We are all constantly making a huge act of faith in others. That's what Jesus wanted, of course. He wanted people to trust him. Many left him that night because they didn't trust him. He said to Peter, 'You go, too.' But Peter said, 'Where would I go? You have the words of eternal life.'

"There's a lot of land to explore near the river. You can see where that takes you. It's colorful down there."

In the afternoon, we lean against a fence under the spruce tree. Ben is wearing lay clothes: his shirt is tucked into his high-waisted pants, so I can see how tiny he is. His belt is very worn, the leather cracking around the buckle. There is a bit of red sauce in his beard. He is speaking of our Irish heritage, how Irish monks conquered Europe.

"They would just get in a boat and see where they landed. Build a monastery there. Then people would gather around them."

People are arriving for mass. Ben's hand shakes dramatically as he holds onto the fence. He loses his balance, takes a step to keep from tipping over. I look at a long hair, lit by the evening sunlight, in his ear.

"Well, how far did you go with the Buddhism?" he asks. "When I was in Tamil land, I found it kind of spooky! Your grandmother tells me you might be getting too Eastern."

I try to explain, but I can see now there is no hope.

"Merton was interested in Buddhism, too, you know," he says. "Meditation is a useful tool, of course, but Buddhism is basically atheist, isn't it?"

"I guess it depends on how you define God."

"The real difference, of course, is the divinity of Christ."

Oh, that! I use simple words, place them humbly in a line: "I understand that as a metaphor. That we are all divine."

"No," Ben says. "That isn't Catholic, that isn't even Christian. There are Christians who think that's true, but they're wrong. The only person who could change the nature of reality is God."

A pause.

"I just don't see where else God would be, if not in everything."

"God is in everything!" We are both looking at the fence-posts, as if God were there in particular. "But not as— not as a person. The important thing is that God became a human person. The whole concept of personhood came from that. Our government is based on that idea."

I see a man of liquid divinity, a God-magnet, highly concentrated with the divinity that is otherwise dispersed evenly throughout the material world.

"Why would there be only one incarnation? Only this one man, so long ago?"

"That is a fundamental mystery. There's mystery in everything. Why are these trees...evergreens? There's mystery everywhere, if you know how to look for it. I mean—how can I move this hand, just with thought?" He holds his hand out, floating it between us in midair. "The idea of personhood is the whole basis of human rights. Look at the human rights situation in India, for example."

"What about the human rights situation here?"

"Well, our society is degenerating, too. But in my day—"

"What about the Native Americans? And slavery? Where was their personhood?"

"There were certainly abuses..."

"Any power based on violence is abusive."

"I agree with you. But I think there are times when it's right to use violence. To defend people, for example."

The sky is growing purple, and the prayer service has come to an end. People are coming out of the chapel, getting into cars and driving away.

"Well, I won't hold you here," Ben says. "But you should think about getting back to your Catholic roots. It's a very visceral thing. It's really the only way."

A strong wish to flee this place, filled now with a dead and stifling No. Even the high corn boasts of Cartesian domination, towering on both sides of the gravel road.

Despair at finging here this narrow-mindedness, this intransigence, this clinging to arbitrary and untenable principles. This belongs among the petty parochial worlds I know only too well, but I did not expect to find it among the Cistercians.

But ask, in what way it is my own narrow-mindedness, my own intransigence with which I am being confronted?

The anger dissipates.

Understanding arrives: my anger is Ben's evangelical fervor.

My No is Ben's No.

It is Inaru's No, too. And Stephen Daedalus's No.

Who knows what a long road this "No" has traveled? Let its journey end here. Let me learn to say yes and no at the same time.

I think of Inaru, surrounded with his ragtag bums, the ugly, the funny-looking people who cling to him. My own mind full of borders and exiles: it is within me that this conflict exists, not elsewhere.

In lay clothes again, Ben looks a bit crazy, his bright eyes shining under his bushy eyebrows.

"We did his blood test," says the woman who was driving. He introduces her as Minh.

"I know your grandmother," she says. "It's very nice to meet you. I'm glad you're here."

"Minh works at the university."

"I was studying to be an architect," she says, "but I went to Italy and things happened. I felt God, and I came back and joined the Church. Your uncle is my spiritual rector." She speaks gently, using her hands. She is dressed in a long skirt and a blouse with a tunic, a pair of fingerless gloves, a head-scarf. "Now I make the religious idols for the monastery. That's how I earn a living. And I work with children. I try to be helpful."

"She took a vow to live only for God. A vow of poverty, a vow of chastity."

"That's not a big change," Minh says, looking me in the eye, "because I live that way anyway. But it's good to take a vow. Then you can be sure of yourself." She makes a fist and claps it into her other hand. "Anyway, I'm glad you're here. Maybe he can teach you something. Sometimes I fight with your uncle because he is so strict. I come from a background where there is not so much pushing. You don't have to use your will—"

"Lax!" Ben interrupts, his eyes flashing.

"But you just go your way naturally," Minh continues, "and your God will find you."

Ben sits across from me in a high-backed chair. He speaks about Nigeria, Congo, Kenya. He tells me about attacks on monasteries, beheadings of monks. I feel something cold on the top of my foot. I kick it away and see that it is a cricket. It flies under Ben's chair, and he moves as if to stomp on it.

"Don't kill it! It's a cricket."

"It's a cricket? Well, I'll let it go on creaking."

More talk of squashing enemies at Vespers.

"The talkers will see!"

I can hear crickets and cicadas through the windows of the chapel. The crucifix is lit golden. Finally, I lean back against the wall, unfold my legs. I look at the statue of the crucified man. Suddenly, inexplicably, it is true. It's both true and untrue. Somehow, I need it to be true. In a way, I believe it.

"May these moments lead to something good, whatever that means, for us, whoever we are."

Everything we do matters, reverberates. A field of yellow flowers: two hawks are circling above the cornfields. I am only what I am. Who knows what I really am?

Mass is long and tedious. Everything is verbalized, and the words make no sense. It's the feast of Saint Augustine. Crisp sunlight, everything dancing outside. I enjoy shaking hands with the big Nigerian monk. I've been looking at him from behind all week, his shiny new belt.

Sally is purchasing one of Minh's icons for her home parish. It's an oil painting of a Madonna and child. Both have large, loving eyes. Their halos are of real gold. Minh handles the painting like a baby—the oil is still wet.

"I don't remember painting it," she says, looking at her work.

"It was all prayer, Minh," Sally says.

Ben reads from the Confessions of St. Augustine and from The Seven Story Mountain of Thomas Merton.

"What is an individual? What is beyond the horizon? What happens after death? The answers to these questions can be life-changing."

I have heard him several times walking along the same roads of thought. Do we simply repeat ourselves? Do we go somewhere else, beyond our speech, leave our bodies here like signposts for the travelers?

In meditation, Ben's face appears before me, vivid. The sky darkens. My vision turns inward. It was wrong, the adult self tells the child self. It's not your fault or theirs. They didn't know. It was an accident.

I hope it's not too late, that I may be there for the ones who need me. It isn't a matter, any longer, of how much tribute I pile up in that gaping chasm.

After the storm, I sit in a quiet, non-discursive state. I feel the hatred as a wave, as a color. Then, the pouring of perfect love into my chest. I am bottomless, and the love keeps pouring into me.

I walk outside and see the stars. The moon is rising, huge, over the cornfields. It must be about two days old.

I wake after a long sleep. In the chapel, the statue of Mary is lit with ecstatic sunlight. I bike down the road. Fields lush in the sunlight, steep hills to swoop down.

As night comes, I hear an inner voice saying my name. It is not a man or a woman's voice. The night is sweet and warm, the moon already high. I begin to pray, or wish, not knowing what words to use.

May the wisdom, compassion, be in me, be in all things. May the children be loved and protected. May the ignorance and suffering be alleviated, may the diseases be cured, may the borders be eased, may the heart be opened.

I pray for whatever I can think of. I feel hope building up in me, hope that comes from asking for something. But what does it mean? Aren't good and bad the same?

This thought has its place, but not here.

Ben expounds on St. Paul, translating from the Latin extemporaneously: "Do not be conformed to this world, but be made new. Pay attention to words. Con-formed. We can be re-formed. At the structural level of the brain, we are constantly being reformed."

He turns the pages of the old book, and I think of the knowledge trickling through the aged brain. He holds his index finger in his cheek. The lines in his brow are beautiful.

We sit in the office. I am alert, awake. There is no more border between us.

He says, "We need a new president. The way he is going over to the Muslims."

I say, "They are right to be upset that they don't have

autonomy in their own countries."

But it doesn't matter. I adore the old man. His robe is dirty, stained grey at the cuffs; there is a spot of green in one place.

"Get in touch with me," he says, "especially if you get into trouble!"

Expect nothing and you will gain everything, writes St. John of the Cross.

St. Paul: In my weakness, I am strong!

I am a ruin, and I let go.

The maidens at the feast that turn to stone in your arms. The world is a puzzle, with its heavens right there among its hells.

Samuel Johnston: "If you set out on the spiritual path to find your true self, you must have faith. You must believe that there is a true self to be found."

We walk Febe to the ravine. Olive is happy, in motion, in jean shorts with poop bags hanging out of her pocket and a dog on a leash.

Olive gets out her bag of paints and images.

In the morning I take Febe to the ravine. I sit among the rocks. It begins to rain. Things can be very beautiful when one is in pain or afraid.

Olive and I sit on the porch. She paints with her poke-berry ink and I sing.

A thinness to reality, a moving-ness. We can go along easily, as if nothing were happening, asleep. I think of those lamp women, sleeping while they wait for the bridegroom. We are like a river, pushed along by currents.

I am closer to love
than the day is to night
should my legs give out under me
and I couldn't get any further
I am still near enough
to see by love's light

I won't need your prayers
you can keep them in the bank
you can keep them in the ground
and if they're just lying around
you can let them lie
my woes are only passing by

8

The wideness of the streets. Dark, Louisiana oaks. Sickness, the song of the highway. Poverty and domination written on the faces of passersby. Blues guitar sliding around like mountains. Victor in soiled waiter's clothes, his desperation thinly covered by a smile.

Coins of rainbow on the table. Sunlight pours through the stained-glass. Oreana and I sit on the porch, enigmas drifting out of our mouths.

I wake up alone. The mind clatters with thoughts. Underneath, the body hums, a part of everything. May I somehow be of help. The sky is painted with clouds.

Prayer creates intention, lifts the heart. I have been unable to see anything worth hoping for.

Preparing for death means detachment from the inner world as well. The horror of death, felt for the other in which one has been dwelling. The primordial and eternal does not die. Where I have been confused, there will merely be a shock of awakening.

Along the road, people with signs stand beside the stopped traffic. In the afternoon heat of the hottest month of the year, their hair burnt, their clothes stale and crackling, their eyes empty and bloodshot.

A homeless man with rotting teeth sits beside me. He tells me about his unemployment check from California, says he is the real son of Queen Elizabeth III.

"You know how she had a stillbirth? That was me and my sister. If she knew I was here telling people this in America, they'd put me in a dungeon. They still have dungeons over there, you know."

I write a poem for a bachelor party. They are all puffing cigars. One of them is standing on top of the prince of England. He looks down at his feet but doesn't seem concerned to see the little toothless man beneath them.

A man has just broken up with the only woman he ever connected with. He is protected, hardened on the outside, even while he says, "I'm thirty-three. It was a nine-month relationship. The longest relationship I've ever been in. It's not easy for me to meet women."

A young man sits beside me and says, "What am I supposed to do? I mean, are we supposed to do something we really enjoy or believe in? We go to college, and then what?"

We listen to WWOZ with the door open to the street. Oreana's Peruvian blankets are bright on the sofas. A siren outside like a quetzal. I am lost, with no ecstasies to chase after. For someone who is willing to suffer, there is only dream.

The pain of displacement. The body does not want to leave its surroundings, which are like its family, its larger body.

I listen to Berenice's old songs. The trombone player kicks his feet, dances in stiff spasms. When the crowd claps, he shouts, "Aw, shut up!" An old, drunken man sits in a daze on the curb, enjoying the music with his whole being. A little girl looks over my shoulder while I type a poem about a young couple's infant son. I let her type. She hits random keys. I ask her to spell her name, but she only knows the first letter. She doesn't recognize the words cat or mom. When I ask her how old she is, she says, "Not five. I was already five."

Laura talks as we walk through the misty after-rain streets. She talks like a road. I listen like flowers on the side of the road, nodding in the breeze, wondering what is under the talking.

The moon keeps following me, peeking out between buildings, over the river. Chartres Street is dark and quiet. A set of antique chairs is illuminated behind a large glass window. I can feel the river over the railroad wall. A boat's tower can be seen above the wharf.

In the empty city, the city with no heart, poverty of love. No nearness, no intimacy, between me and the people around me. Many things I cannot share with them.

Then, I am surprised by Oreana. She is already there, when I reach the other shore.

How did you get here, I wonder. I don't ask.

Within me depths, a long fissure. Ben spoke about how we are changing all the time. I feel my mind growing new memories, new habits.

Big Oreana talks about the Eichman trial, the nature of evil, Heidegger. Then there was laughter—we could feel that the stupor had been punctured, and there was both terror and tenderness in the room. Big Oreana made a groaning sound: "Oh." She was speaking to the terror-beings, saying, "I know you; we are familiar. It makes me sad the way you behave yourselves, but I can see so much right now, I know soon I will understand." She mentions Wendell Berry, a poem about our 'true work'.

"I want to find my work," I say, "but I don't know what it means to be of service."

"It's not that complicated. If you're doing something to liberate someone and to ease their experience of being a human—whether it's teaching them a language or feeding them, just roll up your sleeves and do it."

Oreana and I drive to the lake while the sun is setting. A red gash comes down along the water. In the distance, the sky is streaked with rain.

It is difficult to keep my balance.

I have failed in innumerable ways. I have trampled all over my heart, squandered my gifts, forgotten my duties. It is for this reason that the world is still heavy. It is for this reason that the hollows still howl. It was me and my faulty prayer. It was me, and the tangle of other children with whom I ran.

Watching the clouds change quickly while the rain approaches, I speak with Alex. He felt there was something wrong with him because he's not like other people—he can't focus, can't stay still, can't read. His constant movement, being in the streets, allows him to observe all that's going on around him.

"Most people just imitate other people. It's enough for

them that they've been told what to do. I've been learning to accept that maybe I have my own way of learning, simply by observing."

"When did you start questioning things?"

"Well, all through my twenties. I went from town to town and just worked construction, labor jobs. But I'm not meant to be a laborer, I'm meant to be a caretaker, a mentor. I've been slowly finding that out."

"Were you afraid?"

"I still am. I compared myself to other people. I worried I wasn't what someone would want—what a woman would want."

He speaks about his job at a group home for mentally disabled adults.

"I'd never changed a diaper before, on a baby or anyone. Helping guys take showers, feeding them. Sometimes hand-feeding them. It gets pretty gruesome sometimes."

He explains a disease where the patients pick at their sores, the horrible wounds they cause themselves.

"I'm not sure I could do that."

"I wasn't sure I could, either."

"It means you are an exceptional person."

"Exceptional?"

"Pure. Peaceful within yourself."

"Well, I have my issues. I still have my problems. But this is one thing I can do. And I'm glad I know now I can do it."

He is planning to bike up the West coast to Alaska.

"You're brave," I say.

"It's the same thing as living in one place, really. You still have to survive." He talks about walking around America.

Every town, you find another library. Find water.

I shake water from the boughs of the cypress trees to cool my skin. A huge wall of rain approaches, lightning in it. Water in the grass, in the streets, on the tips of the palm spines, a little gem at each point.

Percy is begging in front of the bike shop. He leaves a pile of unwanted pennies on the concrete inside the gate. A piece of light in the puddle beside the curb shakes, glittering like a jewel. Golden light rests on the power lines and the palm fronds.

What is it that keeps us so blind to the miracle? The universe is always before us, but we push on. We're dogged, we're going to get somewhere.

The sky is purple. The air is sweet. The man under the bridge walks in front of the cars stopped at the light and babbles at me on my bike. Someone yells to him angrily under the bridge: "Come eat your chicken!"

Happiness is not different from other states of agitation. Like sorrow, it must be followed back to its root.

For a moment, I am surrounded by little cherubs—I push them away.

May I see through attachment, I pray. May I ease the suffering in even a small way.

"I just can't stay here," Oreana says. "I don't feel good. I just have to keep moving."

When it rains I keep the doors open, I mop the floor,

clean the surfaces. The house is impossibly filthy, everything shabbily constructed, chronically tainted.

Men are gathered on corners. Sometimes they say, "Hello beautiful," or "What's your name?" The rain has stopped and everything is colorful, glistening. Armstrong park, full of water—fountains, canals. A woman is adjusting her belongings on a bench. I bike to the river, take one photo of the clouds behind the bridge. Rosa's: empty except for the man who always asks for two quarters. I cross over to the Lower Ninth Ward. A woman is driving frantically, smoking, crying, "Where did he go? He took all my money."

Night is falling. At the laundromat a group of men are drinking.

"Come have a beer, baby," one calls to me.

Under the Claiborne bridge, a white egret in a lake beneath the raised road. Rae makes stewed tomatoes with okra. She looks at me in a way that goes right to the belly of the earth. In the past, this look sometimes made me afraid. But most of the shadow beings have evacuated from me now.

We walk along the levee. The dog runs in a swath of green grass.

"The undercurrent in this wind is like Fall," Rae says. "The temperature must not be very high."

Darkness within me, chaos. The world of form is made of this dark chaos, this ignorance. Violence flows from this deep, subconscious stuff. There, beings are distorted, twisted into ourselves.

The wind is blowing. There is power in the night. The trees twist at their hips, the lines in the bark open. I can smell the oldness of the houses. Someone practicing a trumpet, a flood of voices in the open door of a bar.

Drums in Armstrong Park, in the shade of the huge trees, the air misty and sparkling. A blond woman is dancing with an old woman with long dreadlocks in African dress. They take off their shoes.

The older woman beckons to me, saying, "I need some ladies. This is a dance from the Congo."

I feel like a newborn. I am standing in a circle of women of many colors and nationalities. She teaches us movements, how to respond to the drummers. She tells us to take partners. I am paired with a shy young pregnant woman. In closing, one by one we salute the drummers with improvised movements. I am surprised at myself for going to the center of the circle.

After the dance is finished, the woman in white addresses the group. This gathering is to honor the woman who was the one teaching us the dance. People tell her how important she is to them and the community, and she gives thanks. She speaks about being a nurse, and how much of her life she spent "treating sick."

"That's part of it," she says, "But I want to be a healer. I want to keep people healthy. I tell people to move, even if it's just a little. To eat a little better. Then you don't end up with all the problems I have. Be a better you, that's what I tell them."

A carnival beat. A tiny child sits at a huge djembe and

hits it with his tiny hands. He gets excited when the beats become fast and high; he starts drumming faster, too.

The woman in white picks up a shaker. Another woman pours out a bottle of agua de florida. A woman in a light, billowing green dress comes into the circle and dances with grace and beauty.

"Let's do it. Come on. What, you scared?"

She lifts her mother from the wheelchair. They dance together. I close my eyes. I am pure feeling.

A fat man singing operatically at intervals, sitting on the curb.

"Understand it better by and by," sings the banjo player.

The wounded child deep in my trunk. The shadow in me—anger-hatred, in a place near the skull. The outer layer of the brain. A place of ugliness, immobility.

Another being toward the back of the mind. Spacious, fluid, relaxed. I rock back and forth between the two. My left side with a solid, all the way down to my heel.

I pray for love to dissolve the obscurations. Seeing the body as the world—Oreana as being in my own body. Everything in it, pouring in.

For a moment, with my eyes closed, I feel the true absence of self. When I listen carefully, the anger is sorrow. Someone is crying. What is she crying about?

For a moment, I see clearly that there is no 'I.' I see the space, the room, where the voices, characters, are scattered around. Then I am overpowered again by the habits, the tide of strong tendencies. The vision is covered up.

Heaviness, solidity. The dream where I am trying but cannot. Trapped in form.

Lying under the tree, the water birds picking in the mud. The lavender lady playing the finger piano, singing on Royal Street. The Quarter alive, bustling.

Feelings of solidity, nearness again. Ducks in the fountains. Homeless people waking up, beginning their lives in beauty. A runaway in my mind, pulling up weights.

The taut roads to loss, they won't slacken for two days now.

Loneliness.

"Solitude is the measure of one's capacity for intimacy."

Oreana: "I have so much to tell you!" She's excited. She says, "Corn tortillas in the morning! It's what you're supposed to do." She unleashes a storm of words, thoughts. "I need people! I love these mornings!"

My face frightens me in the morning light. The formations as objects. Subjectivity in the spaciousness around them.

I feel anger crawling through me.

Where did you crawl out of? I ask the anger. That's ok, go on your way.

"You look well," Sonya says twice.

We talk like wells. We talk about our pain without mentioning it. Her pain and my pain, holding hands. Her lips are red with lipstick. She's come out, forced herself to come out, telling herself she wouldn't have to talk to anyone.

"People are terrifying," she says. "I'm going through a second adolescence. It hurts."

Olive and I sit by the bayou.
"What have you been doing?"
I'm lost. It seems nothing is happening.
"I'm beginning to feel landlocked," I say.
"You're not landlocked at all!"
I wonder if anything I've done has made any difference. Olive says teaching is the highest form of giving.
"It's giving of yourself."

Mind disordered, angry. Ducks, a hawk casually hunting squirrels. I meditate on the side of the pond. A lamppost undulates in the water.

My heart begins to leave again. I don't see signs of myself in my actions. The parks and boulevards have lost their innocence.

"It's not you," I say again. I look into the water, streaked yellow and blue.

"These dragonflies," Olive says. She is speaking from the bowels of eternity.

She begins to play "Do You Know What It Means" on the ukelele.

I sit by the river where the barges dance a slow ballet.
Dorothy comes and sits down beside me.

"Whatcha readin'?"

"Faulkner. Wild Palms." I show her the jacket.

Dorothy nods.

"That about palm reading?"

"No, it's about—I'm not really sure yet. I just started it."

"You not working tonight? They got a lot of people out there."

"No..."

"You don't got some change? I wanna get some beignets."

I smile and give her a five dollar bill.

"You don't want to go together? We could share them."

"If you eat the fruits of this world, you risk losing your connection to the other world. Stay empty a while, remember your dreams."

Oreana cooks omelets. She is soft and lovely in her pajamas. The dancing light. The coffee cups.

Walking in the park, we see palms, moss-covered cypresses. The water is filled with birds, turtles. Halloween decorations are appearing.

"The charnel ground is coming," I say.

"Think of the death of your sorrow," Oreana says.

I grow toward the light of my opposite, my hero-mask.

At the church, they love Olive. Pinar says, "Que preciosa tu hermana."

Juan says, "Olive is a vegetarian. That's why she is so beautiful."

"The rivers are all dry in Nicaragua," Pinar says. Drought: sequía.

"Life is complicated there," Juan says. He was a nurse in the hospital for three years. But working construction here, he can support his two younger brothers in school.

A drizzly Sunday. The Quarter is empty of tourists, but there is a gentle flow of walkers. A drunk man says, "I'm not drunk. I had surgery on this hip." He pulls a bottle of liquor from his pocket. "I haven't even started drinking this yet!" There are diamonds in the pavement. The lunatics are warming themselves by the music.

I heard the anger in the highway song. It was my own anger, insisting on getting somewhere, now. Olive buys a bottle of wine and a box of Cheez Its. It rains in the dark. I write a poem for a French girl who is going to see her lover in China. Filling the broken cup.

Olive feeds a Cheez It to the baby cockroach.

"He should put the tomato with it," she says.

Let the rivers be wet again, let the rivers be full.

It will work when you get out of the way.

We ride down Esplanade. I take Olive's photo in the dazzling sunlight.

"Look to the right," I say.

We pass glittering mansions along the bayou. Cypresses, palmettos. At the lake, we read a grave marker. The words have been scratched onto a piece of cement. "Te quiero, papa," it reads at the bottom.

"Everyone born must die. Everyone met must be separated. Everything created must be destroyed."

"I have noticed that sometimes I am suddenly angry at someone, but I do not have the causes of anger. I can see that my mind is clear, but anger is arising anyway. That is karma. That is karma from the past spontaneously ripening."

My heart blushes under the new moon.

Olive is gone. Sadness lies in the canyon of the way things were.

Oreana and I move to a new house. I weep in the back yard, listening to the sounds of the air-conditioners.

I return to the lake. Dragon-flies swarm around me. While the sun sets, it becomes clear.

There are two tensions: pride and attachment.

"I better swim," I say out loud.

I tire quickly.

I ride home through the darkening cypress trees. It is possible to let go.

I tell Rae about the three non-virtuous mental states: harmful thoughts, emotional blind spot, craving. The five poisons.

"I think some of that is biological," she says.

"Yes, but DNA is also our karma. We are our DNA, and we have been acting this way, selfishly, for many lifetimes. So if we want to evolve, it will take many more lifetimes. Infinite lifetimes."

"It sounds hard," she says. She understands.

It is I who have been paralyzed, who have neglected my

inner lights. I am haunted by the injustice in every fiber of this world. I am like a wooden doll stuck in a stiff pose, while action is required.

How is it that I am supposed to be living? What is the real work?

I am weighed-down by tendencies and formations. I find it difficult to disentangle myself from a self-image, an old story.

If I were clean, I would be able to laugh at the reflections. But I am still embodying them—numbness, destructiveness, pride.

Inviting divinity to inhabit me. Inviting the heart to wake up, compassion to arise.

The false assumption that others will notice what I am doing. There is only one witness, the one that has seen all. "You who wove me in the womb."

Does this witness forgive me? Could this witness still love me? This question is at the center of my despair, my need for approval—the need for my flawed self to be absolved by my higher self—to be forgiven.

Even if anyone should grant me what I seek, I would not be able to accept it without the forgiveness of that one.

The teacher says, "Don't attach. The mind is free already. Imagine you are the supreme God. How would you feel? You get dignity. Then it is very easy for you to detach from negative influences." He speaks about freedom from dualistic thinking. Good and evil, progress and stagnation. "May all beings be enlightened," the Rinpoche says, "in this lifetime."

I feel invincible, dignified. The lake is full of wild waves. A cold front is coming. I am finished with thinking, planning, ideas. I connect to the part of me that only exists, exists and does not make efforts. The part that knows, knows.

The music is painfully beautiful, the poems wrenching my guts. I rock and close my eyes like a maniac. The tuba player jumping out of his instrument and bellowing "Amazing Grace" into the street. Currents of ecstasy among the walkers in the street. They dance, stroll, exchange looks with one another. Is this heaven always here?

Amar tells a story of two brothers, a long allegory about cowboys on a farm. Percy walks up on his crutches. Amar runs inside and comes back out with a banana and coke.

"Alright, thank ya," Percy says, and rows away.

"You used to be a revolutionary," Amar says.

"I want to be a revolutionary again."

"I know, I know," he says. "Forget it, you will be a revolutionary again."

"I'm so confused," I say. "There is this surface appearance. Everything is fine. People are shopping. But underneath, so much horror. So much pain."

"I think that's part of why people come here. To forget."

For a moment, we are here, having been spared, ludicrously, until another moment. The moment we are in becomes at once trivial and large.

"Do you ever think about the people? They come and go, they pass by. They never stop coming! It's like an endless stream. Like a river. You know, to them, we're fascinating."

A carriage goes by with a made-up lady and a man riding

in it. A group of women pass by on foot.

Peter says, "You are a writer."

But is that something to be?

We watch the street for a moment in silence upon the slate tiles.

"When people get depressed, there's nothing anyone can say," Peter says. "But I'm glad you're here. You made my day."

I try to stay until eight, but I can't wait. I stoop down in Pirate's Alley, between the cathedral and the book shop, and cry into my knees.

"It's normal," Amar says. "First you become a teenager, then a young woman, then an experienced woman. You think, 'I'm twenty something years old, I'm not married, I'm not with baby, but I want to go to Europe, but I want to come back from Europe.' It's not just you. It's everyone."

He brings me napkins. He waits. He leans against the building with his feet up.

"In a way, I'm glad you're crying," he says. "It means you're not satisfied. You know, McDonald's comes with fries and a coke, and it's filling, but it's not satisfying. That's why people are hungry day after day, whether they have it or not."

I cry before him as if he were a shrine.

A blind man feels his way up to the curb. Amar jumps nimbly to move the sign out of his way. His movement is swift, essential, selfless.

Returning, he says, "A sand castle can so easily wash away. Any wave can knock it down. Be like a rock. Not much fancy this and that. Not much moving around. Be like an eagle. The pigeons are beautiful, but they are always in a group. The eagles—so high. Maybe only one or two.

"You're in the best place in the world right now. Remember the story? The Rumi story I told you? You don't remember?

"The caravan was going through the desert, and they found a well. They lowered their bucket to get water, but when they pulled the rope up, the bucket was gone. Somebody or something cut the bucket.

"So they tried it a second time. Again, they pull up the rope and the rope has been cut. So a wise guy says, 'Tie me to the rope and lower me down and I will see what's going on like that.' So they tie him and lower him down. He gets to the bottom of the well and down there's a cave-man.

"He says, 'I'm going to ask you a question. If you answer right answer you can take water in your bucket, go free. If you answer wrong, I cut you up. Here's the question: Where is the best place in the world?'

"I'm asking you now."

I hesitate.

"Answer, or I'll cut you up. Rumi is asking you. Hafez is asking you."

"Right here?"

"I cut you up! You're wrong. But the wise guy answered right. He said the best place in the world is where you have a friend. The cave man untied him, he let him go free. That's where you are. The best place in the world.

"I do see differently than you," Amar says. "I see a light at the end of the tunnel. In politics, in the world. In you. Your words, your art, your thoughts, the way you're bringing it out. Please let me cook something for you."

I nod.

"Thank you."

He kisses my cheek and goes inside. The sweeper sweeps around me. Amar comes back and brings me through the kitchen.

"There's a girl in here, somebody I'm helping out. Come on, I'll introduce you."

He brings the food and sets a table. A beautiful young woman is sitting on his couch, moving slowly, in a dazed way, choosing music to play on her phone. She has long wavy blond hair and an open, boyish face. A necklace is hanging from her neck, between the buttons of her denim shirt. Her fingernails are painted black, and the black nail-polish bottle is on the table beside her. A notebook is lying beside her on the couch, and Shabazz, the cat, is curled up beside her.

"Megan," Amar says. "Megan."

Amar sets before us plates of fish and potatoes. I notice how his spirit is like a wide tent, sheltering many souls.

I look at the masks on the walls: women's faces waking out of petals, blossoming out of opening layers, pieces of molds breaking away to either side. Aging is the constant shedding of selves—but always there is another mask beneath the mask that peels away. The seer, the eye, remains, empty, formless.

We watch a documentary about birds. Amar and Megan fall asleep. I am the only one still awake as the British naturalist muses, "Why do they all sing at dawn? It's a cold time, so for many birds, there is nothing to eat. Perhaps they might as well sing."

Sitting in one place
I am crucified by change
by time

battered by the caravan
of wandering winds,
by rain and shine

my poems are the orchid's blood
in the apron of the road
my sighs and cries are sundered gutters
in the path of roots grown swollen

in this trunk there is no place
only that which can't be named
a dancer on death's floating stage
all her footprints washed away

then you've never left at all
pacing in your sacred cage
borderless, nowhere to fall
what to say then,
where to fade

9

My scratches on the deep belly of oblivion. The young man who sweeps has his drawings spread out around him. Later, I watch him stock the drink coolers.

A long-haired man in a cowboy hat is playing slow electric guitar. The opera singer is performing. The tarot reader has a station set up on the empty crates. He looks fresh and cool, as if he slept indoors last night.

Papery feelings in the papery light. Brown sycamore leaves on the ground, the smell of sweet burning, like brewing molasses.

Roundedness of thinking. Whatever I think, the opposite is also true. The union of emptiness and form, relative and ultimate. Near the water, the cages fall away. I know I am leaving. I am pure, without coarse identity—free? I cry for joy, thinking of everything, thinking of my heart, of the ones I love. Even the quibbling, neurotic thoughts have their loveliness. Even the strong cords of attachment are expressions of bliss. The luminous self, the ingenious, laughing child, the heart that rains gifts.

Thoughts as objects—objects of perception. Then what remains that is subject? On Royal Street, a shirtless man in a top-hat, skull and bones chalked on the front, plays a bass made out of a sink basin. A man wheels out an upright piano and plays it in the street in front of Rouse's.

Sandiman reads my orphaned poem.

"I like it," he says. "But I don't know. It seems sort of sad."

"The topic was 'being directionless.' I think a lot of people feel that way."

He nods. "I feel that way sometimes. The other day, I took acid at four in the morning and tripped until midnight the next day. A lot of the time I was in my mind thinking, 'I'm bad.' The next day I went walking in the Quarter. I had four stones with me. I gave away three stones, and I looked at my reflection in a window. I looked like a crazy hobo. I had to get out of the Quarter.

"I walked down this street and I was talking to myself the whole way. I went to yoga at my friend's house, and while I was doing yoga, I felt like I had to cry. Two tears came out: one from each eye. I thought about whether I should break down or hold it in, but in the end, I held it in.

"I used to sell my art on the ground right here. I would stay up all night and sleep by the river. But then I got a house, a car. I feel trapped. I don't feel motivated. I'm twenty-five now."

I can smell him: essential oils and copper wire.

"This summer I was in Vermont. It was cold and raining all the time. I wasn't making jewelry. I was smoking three times a day and just getting more depressed."

I say, "Beneath all that, your pure self is always there. The rest can just fall away."

"You know, I used to say a lot of things. But I realized, it's easy to say things. It's hard to do things. I guess I learned my lesson. I probably deserved it."

Loosening where the mind has been clenched, keeping me reigned in, reserved, correct. Habits of self-editing.

Depression-waves around the roof of the brain. Perhaps it is true, as Gabilan said, that I am attached to my unhappiness.

"It's all labeling."

Difficult to let things change, not to become fixed. Difficult to keep letting go, each time I think I know.

Others feel it. How do we get through all this change? Every moment, we are reborn into a painful world. We keep creating the world we are in. We prove too weak to maintain the clear light. We return to our desire, flee from our terror, set the wheel spinning.

Sandiman sits in the shade, I sit in the sun. He seems to be at rest, like the waves, free from hate, petty prejudices. Then, a hint of violence. Like everyone, he keeps changing.

All the others are me.

We lie on the concrete steps. Sandiman moves closer to me. I sit up in meditation posture. Sandiman sits a few feet away. I try to maintain equanimity, but there is tension in my mind. I am attached. This femaleness, this animalness. It comes in softly, dilating my veins, putting a pillow over everything and under everything. A stupid, animal thing. It seems subtle and delicate, but it is greedy and volatile. It ties traps of special attachment, becomes wild when they are evaded.

I sit back in my body and watch the female feelings billowing near the front.

All the others are me. I feel this other body, something

like a soul, like a little idol, hidden in my tree trunk. This little soul is someone I can help.

She begins to relax. What a relief! This dictator has been punishing me, sending me plagues. She does this because she is in pain. I can take away her pain and give her my peace.

Aliveness. Forms like ruins that have been left to deteriorate. Without breath, rebirth, they disintegrate. The innocence of even the obscurations. They have traveled a great distance and have changed along the way. Their origin is in a child, a sweet and pure nature.

"I can't stop thinking," Sandiman says.

"It's not always easy," I say. "We go through phases."

I hug him goodbye. He kisses my collarbone. I don't look at him as I begin to walk away.

Joey says, "Hey. I know, you went on an airplane."

"But I'm back now."

"Yeah."

"Where do you want to go?"

"To the jungle?"

I call the train a crocodile.

"No, it's a train! This isn't the jungle."

I put him in the seat of the grocery cart.

"This is fun!"

"Yeah!"

He helps me put the groceries on the counter. He helps me put away the cart. He pushes the unlock button on the car keys.

At home I pour him orange juice.

"This is good!"

I put the mattress down and we jump on it. I make monkey sounds and he attacks me with pillows. I wheel him around the house upside down.

"I'm upside down, I'm upside down!" he says, laughing, elated.

He holds Oreana's shirt in front of the fan and watches it undulate.

"I'm cleaning this for Aunty Ory," he says.

He plays with everything, seeing what it will do, what it will look like.

At the lake I chase him around the playground with a banana peel. I hold him while he walks on the mossy concrete steps. At home he plays with the bike pump. Pressing the nozzle to himself, he says, "This could make me really big."

We sleep briefly. I start to cook beans and rice. When Joey wakes up, he says, "I want my mommy."

I get out the typewriter. He writes Eva a letter.

"These are mommy's words!"

We sit on the front porch.

"Dime algo," the neighbors call to him.

Self-cherishing attitude, tight. I breathe into it, offer it love, appeasement. I watch it grow, sit up. A giant, tent-like body erecting.

I bring the black table to the street with me and cover it with the wrap skirt. Berenice is playing. The tarot reader is burning sage.

When I arrive the front door is closed. I consider

escaping but knock, enter. I look at Sandiman, a glass of wine in his hand.

"You made it!"

I move toward him, but the couch is in the way, people are crowded around.

I hide my face with my sleeved hands.

"Come on, let's get you some wine," he says. I walk behind him down a narrow passage. He has a handkerchief in his back pocket. He pours me a glass of wine. In the courtyard, there is a small fire in a ring of stones.

"Nice," I say. Everyone keeps saying, "Nice."

A projector plays colorful designs on the wall. We watch the fire.

"You never slept on the river sands?" Sandiman asks with surprise.

"No! There are some rough characters out there."

I hold my glass of wine like a lamppost in a strong wind. I am self-conscious.

We go inside, where his artwork is displayed. The centerpiece is a crown of wire and stones. It sits on a pillow, other wire-wrapped stones hanging from fishing line above it. His rings are on goblin-like hands made of thick dark wire, his necklaces resting on antlers.

"Do you know what a nautilus is? They were all female. When you're holding it, you're holding something four million years old."

I find myself talking, saying things I don't mean.

We walk down Royal Street, looking into gallery windows. A painting of a donkey. A sculpture of a fat man in a business suit lying prostrate.

"This is not a sight people want to see," Sandiman says. "There are a lot of people who look like this in this city. And this is what they look like dead."

A mummy sitting in the window seat at Muriel's.

"That guy's having a good meal," Sandiman says.

A building has collapsed on Royal Street. The block is barricaded. Sandiman asks the police man what happened as we exit the partitioned area.

"It fell down. And you decided to walk through the danger zone. It could have kept falling on you."

"How did it fall?"

"It just decided to fall. Two hundred years is a long time. It stood as long as it could."

"Have a good night," Sandiman says earnestly.

Bare mannequin necks in a jewelry store window. I count the rings on Sandiman's hands: seven. Four bracelets.

"I don't wear that much jewelry anymore," he says.

We sit in a circle of light on an empty stage. A cop shoos us off. We take Bourbon Street, full of dazed people.

"This never gets old." Sandiman says. "I like it here because I know people with money and people with nothing. Those guys at the gallery are realtors, they sell houses. But I know a lot of people who have no money."

"We're all connected."

"Did you read that somewhere?"

The pain is here. Sitting in the yard, the feeling of pain, woundedness, obscuration, flowing out of a place in my left side, an endless stream of smoke being carried by the wind. I watch it unfurling, seemingly without end.

The belief that I am not good is also a belief that no one is good, that nothing is good. It is violence against existence.

The bottle-cap tap-dancing children pass by. A drunk sleeps, sprawled on the sidewalk all afternoon. Bubbles rain from a balcony. People take pictures. A second-line passes, feathers fluttering at the edges of white parasols.

Stepping out of attachment but allowing the relative world to continue its play, a necessary expression of the ultimate world.

Am I the only one who is deluded? There is so much space—the air lifting women's hair, sunlight showering indiscriminately. Isn't every particle of falling sun enlightened? The serene smiles of passersby.

Berenice striking in the sunlight. The drummer shakes his head in ecstasy. The crowd cheers, everything lifts for a moment.

Looking for the looker. Praying for transcendent wisdom. Aware of obstacles.

Noise, the culmination of mistaken views and actions, an eruption of afflictions. This flesh is a very old story, but I can let it go.

If we can help one another awaken, then we will be real. If we can help one another help the whole, then we have meaning.

In my mind, this knot, this tangle. But in the world, there is no knot, no tangle.

The sickness will pass like other sicknesses—with time.

I see all the people I know. What are they really like, under their forms? The souvenir shop lady brings me a cup of cool water, candied pecans, a handful of Halloween candy. Desire caused this problem and that problem. Sometimes I feel so gentle and big, but moments later, I'm small and jagged.

On the boat, lights and waves, the voices of the passengers, the nonsense murmurs of the sea and of all my thoughts, my moods that pass like weather. Everything sensible turns to waves. I sit back, touching and being touched by all. I recognize the extraordinary. The long roads these moments have traveled on.

Berenice teaches the tourists how to die, how to shout when someone has crossed the river, which horn blast means they've reached the other shore. The band plays "Lonesome Walk With Thee," then "When the Saints Go Marching In." And he is there, smiling in the sun, the golden one.

I haven't even begun to disappear. In the realm of the gods, there is a pillow between all the hard surfaces, so that one floats. When any kind of rub arises, there is big panic. And this river of words? A river of stasis. The way things are, a rolling rock, an object in motion.

Don't try, Seymour says. If you try, it will just be luck. When the spirit wants to move, there is no luck. Let me not try. Let me not use an 'if.'

"It seems like other people know," Roberto says. "But nobody knows. It's hard to believe that nobody knows, because everybody fakes a little bit."

Emptiness even in the thoughts.

A man comes over to see: is it the woman of my dreams? No, it's not she.

The wisdom is already here, even the pain is soft, soft.

The sea, the sea. She really is calling, and I really do hear.

Someone showed me a point of light. Here, daughter. These are your roots for heating. This is the purple hall of your jade city. This is heaven, where the lions and lambs are nuzzling.

All my mothers, most of them dead. All my fathers, enemies, friends, most of them dead. Only this tiny illuminated circle in the great field of shades.

I am purified, without any more debt, the effects of me balanced out. What does that look like?

I sit with the question, but the answer does not emerge.

The vast space around us is also us. The vast time around us is also us.

Can you imagine if all the material was awake? We wouldn't have to kill and eat. You would float into yourself like a cloud.

"I am nourished by pure essences."

I'm still able to be disappointed, still keeping hidden motives, despite the daily relinquishing of grasping and delusion.

He's hiding in a sea grape tree.

"Can you hear the water?"

In the sun, I looked at Amar's tired eyes. He said it's not enough. Only revolution is enough.

"We are responsible for ourselves. If everybody is doing the wrong thing, we are still responsible for our own action. When you get off this merry-go-round," he says, gesturing toward Mimi's.

"What merry-go-round?"

"The world! Life! Whatever it is. The universe is expanding. Everything you do lasts forever."

I can only sit with the emptiness for a moment. Then it's back to animal doing.

Having lain my troubles down, I go back into the old haunts, so full of love it hurts.

I have been dead before, before being born, and it didn't hurt. We grow up and become confused. Actually, we can stand anything.

A very soft presence with me these days. The spaciousness that contains the forms. Neutral, listening, knowing. She doesn't judge, simply observes. She sees the artifice for what it is, holds it like an object in her hand.

A washboard player from other times is back in town. He speaks a strange English, intentional and kind. Loneliness under things. Movement in the mind, slipperiness, guilt making things wild. Where it hurts, where there is a tattered edge, that is where I connect, where I am real.

Halos: roundedness. The rounded person, complete.

I write a poem for a boy diagnosed with leukemia at six.

"Sometimes I'm a little bit glad I got cancer," he said. "I've met so many nice people."

He plays the banjo, always wears a cowboy hat.

I write for a woman's 60th birthday.

"My mother died at 58," she says.

In a deep place, with the painted curls of thangka clouds, there is still attachment. The bloody, biological mind. That mind is tied to the Tibetan clouds, too.

The divine can still love the mundane; the mundane is the divine, in a twisted shape. I feel the twistedness of my own shape, the bend in it.

Big Oreana: "We are concerned we are not worthy because we are separate from God. I can't separate myself from guilt. I've tried. It's always going to be there. But I can recognize it. At least it's not 24-7. Where I have guilt, that's where I can connect to the suffering."

This has all been the same dream: the dream that nothing moved.

I feel the cold air on my skin, the mind moving like a leopard in a jungle. But do I really feel it?

It is happening, and it is not happening.

Royal street is confused. There is no band. A bum is sleeping under a blanket on the corner. A man in a wheelchair holds a cardboard sign. A man in a Saints jersey poses like a statue.

The last rush of warmth in a weeping grey November. Brilliant clouds moving through this beloved corridor of sky, A darkness within me, a well-worn sorrow. I am leaving town the day after tomorrow.

A woman with tight boots passes by with her husband. Sedentary people, synthetic clothes and bloodstreams.

I watch the people. How to describe them? The women put on a strange, frantic show. The men keep their show somewhere in the ether, in cyberspace or some other world.

The tap-dancer children lean on me, type their names.

Children in the streets selling M&Ms.

"Want to buy some candy?" They ask the wrong people—the vendors, the homeless people, the musicians. They don't even claim to be raising money for a cause. A teenager is in charge of four or five little ones.

The universe has her knife to my throat. All these human sacrifices walking around, freshly waxed. A man in a wheelchair drifts up and down the block. Now and then he mumbles about a dollar for something in the store.

All the flowers seem to be wilting. It is perhaps things ending that I feel, the truth coming out.

We're in a sacred world
we're on a sacred street
and sacred are the sounds unfurling
achingly they're sweet

from that broken set of pipes
that gust of vagrant wind
the broken places in the sidewalk
let the sunshine in

this ground's been paved by empires
but she is still alive
beneath her mask of armor
like the rest, she's made of light

you'll end up in love one day
you needn't even try
just candy castles in the way
the flood will lick aside

10

Tiny boxlike houses, miniature palm and banana trees. I change into a dress in the airport bathroom, ask taxi attendants where to go, walk in the heat and sunlight. I switch from train to bus. On Highway 1, I begin to hitchhike. A truck pulls over. The driver is a big Cuban man with a scar on his right cheek, light eyes, a mystical smile. He gives me a cold diet iced tea.

"No sugar, no nothing!" he says. "I love Cuba! Cuban music? The best! I live here twelve years. But I love Cuba."

He doesn't make me speak. I am grateful to ride in silence. He lets me off. From there I ride with David, an Army veteran with a memory problem and agoraphobia. He is on his way home from his weekly VA appointment in Miami. He tells me stories about Steve Jobs and lets me off before the 7-mile bridge in Marathon. Joe picks me up: a leathery-faced Cuban man with a hearing aid. He shouts when he talks.

"Yeah, I like to go to Key West and see some music. Go to the Green Parrot and smoke a little pot! They won't let me go to Cuba. They don't want Cuban nationals unless you're going visit your family there. They won't let me go on my sailboat. They won't let me fly there."

Three guys pick me up. One of them has something wrong with him—perhaps he is being conned by the other two. His arm is too small for his body. He asks me nice questions, but his eyes are not nice. The one in the back seat leans across the seats. Sometimes he forgets what I have already said, and other times he remembers things I had forgotten I'd mentioned. The driver throws a pack of cigarettes to the convicts on the road gang.

"Yep, he tapped his watch. That means he got it."

The trees are exquisite, blue-green on a cloudy day. Tiny yards. Lushness, tropical lushness everywhere.

Ana, Gabilan and Andres are on the porch. Tula is there, her hair curly, crawling around.

Gabilan says: "Poet! You look like a homeless person!"

I set my bags down. Fena leans down to hug me. Everything is buzzing, a sheen over things.

"So you wanna take a nap and we can make some hotdogs later?" Gabilan says.

The eternal youth of Gabilan—he is happiest when everyone is together.

I take a nap in Tula's room. Ana is taking a driving test on the computer. My pulse is thick. I can't sleep. When I come out, Fena is sitting on the steps, burnishing her beads.

"So what are you gonna do?" she asks.

"I have to make a plan."

"You have to make a plan so you can not follow it?"

I lie down in the abandoned school. The sky is full of drifting hawks. The wet sky, the palms and vines, the hawks. A man walks up.

"How you doing, sweetheart? I live here."

"Is it ok if I sit for a while?"

"Sure. Sometimes I find people camping out here. If it's nighttime I let them stay, but then I kick them out in the morning."

He goes into a door. I begin writing, but soon I lie down. The sun comes out of the clouds and burns my skin, but I don't move.

Inaru's truck, a hammock hanging in the cab. The seats are gone. He parks at Oscar's, says he slept in this parking lot last night.

Nothing moving forward. The arrest. Gabriela has been kidnapped.

He says, "I'm in exile. I'm not the real thing for everybody any more. I lost my special privileges. I could cry about it, but."

His skin is taut and ashy. He speaks of health problems, paranoias.

"I thought you were going to do something. All of your plans."

"It's just so easy. I want to get a big pile of money together."

In a cool blue back yard, he pulls the fruits from the trees. Full of doubts, but I can't do any better than try. I am willing to be wrong.

He sings as we are leaving, "Oh, Susana!"

I put Tula to sleep and walk her up and down the block, humming. She buries her face in my chest. The wind blows over us. The roots of Tula's consciousness, growing here on my heartbeat.

Gabilan builds a fire. Fena makes skewers with squash, zucchini, and tomatoes. Tula crawls around in the leaves. I keep moving her away from the fire.

I read Roque Dalton verses on the drizzly porch. I meet Ana. George is playing, big and bearlike in his African shirt. Elina from Hungary dances gracefully. You can see that she was a ballerina. A bum and a tourist dance in their underwear for a table full of women.

Waking in the unfinished room, I look for the frequencies of love in the world, in my cells. It is difficult to love myself. I am guilty. I see ignorance, craving and aversion spinning around, a little knot within me.

Disordered. Everything bends. Mimi in the kitchen: her long black wing of hair, her black eyeliner. I feel old and ridiculous beside her flawless beauty. She has washed all the dishes.

Fear of what people will think.

"The easiest way to ease suffering in yourself is to reach out to someone else who is suffering."

Samantha is worried. Her stomach hurts. We walk with Tula. At the house, Fena offers us Chinese food. She says, "I'll get it this time, and you can get it when you're working." I am touched.

I hold a tangle of wooden toys before Tula, making them clatter. I clap my hands and she claps her hands. She looks at me in wonder. Ana dazed on the couch. She makes kissing faces at Tula, holds her in her motherly arms.

"This island is full of people who are not moving forward," Samantha says. "Fena and Gabilan are the only ones who seem to be moving."

As I move about, the breathiness begins to harden. It is not easy to love the small motions, not easy to stay lovingly awake. The day is hot and dazzling. I love, but beneath my optimism, there is fear.

Gabilan is finishing the room. I move my things to the porch. I'm feeling cloudy and staid. I sweep the roof, we open the tent.

My mind is pointed to an inner question. I have arrived here, but I am lost.

Gabilan asks, "Are you really going to be ok up here again?"

The Poinciana tree has grown while I was away. Gabilan pulls its branches and twists off the ends. Fena comes out with a long espresso for me and a coffee with milk for Gabilan, then bikes off to work. Samantha walks me to work with Tula in the stroller. I sit in the old poetry station, making no money, watching the parade of tourists pass by.

I sit at Dog Beach, the mother-consciousness hearing the small neurotic self flail about. The hearer hears everything, is a backdrop for the one who makes the noise. I wish for the two to meet.

Hurting without a reason. The need to matter, the need to be loved. An old abyss opens. Be like the river. Be with the river. Get there another way, if there is resistance here. Adam got in another accident, lost all his money again. Everything is repeating.

Tula is asleep on Samantha's chest. She puts her perfectly down into her crib. Later Gabilan gives Tula a bath in the cooler. She catches the water he pours in her mouth.

I walk with Ana to see the chalk drawings. The weather has changed. It's all I can do to push the baby carriage.

I move into the still, silent place in the belly. Who is making all this noise? The mental activity has a location. It is on the right side, in the back. There are other activities going on in other places. There is the place that says, "This is not good enough." A counterpoint, the voice that says, "I am ok, no matter what." This part of the mind has a water-faucet smile, buddha-smile. On the left side, in the back. A fear-voice, the voice of death, that finds a precipice of ruin in everything. This is a frontal voice.

These mental activities surround the center of the brain like a wreath or a crown. From the center, I send them love. I accept them all, welcome them.

Thanksgiving. Ana makes macaroni and cheese. Fena at the hot plate warming tortillas. I carry Tula. She slaps things to see what they sound like.

At times I catch my mind in an act of recrimination.

"You hurt me," my mind says. But I am choosing to be hurt.

Panic about money. Some days I earn nothing at all. The weather remains cold and windy. I am plagued by memories.

I sit in front of the red brick wall they say Hemingway built himself to keep tourists out. There is a piece of sky and above a carved white fence stretch palms and flower bushes and white wooden houses with tin roofs.

Tourists appear in waves. One day there are Indians in the street, the next day, Germans. A group of Estonians say that according to Hemingway, every sea port in the world boasted at least one Estonian.

It rains Poinciana leaves. Sadness, a guest I treat with respect.

A yellow truck goes by. The yellow truck is almost nothing. The afternoon is sinking into oblivion, taking with it the Poinciana leaves and Inaru on his tricycle: a boy with a rusted sword in his hand.

He cuts me a coconut. I look in his eyes as I receive it from him.

I feel lonely and un-useful. There is so much pain—but I am merely acting out "pain." How can I use this pain to heal others?

All night, Poinciana rain on the tarp. The tiny leaves— yellow, speckled green. Visions of myself grown old. But perhaps I am already old. It is not a warning about the future, but a warning about the present.

I have been waiting for the fates to speak to me, for the bugles to call out loudly. But the world has been talking to me all along. The world does not use any other tones than trumpets. When she speaks, she speaks loud and clear. Truly, she has never stopped speaking.

Lying in the sand, I thank my feet. I'm sorry I insulted them. They are not mine but ours, borrowed to help us walk forward.

"I feel like we are walking a path," Sue said. Who are we, then, who are walking together? Who are we but God?

This coin of white light in me. She does not participate in time or space, eventualities or human dramas.

I will have to learn it: everything joined must be parted.

I recognize the pain. It has an end, like any storm, like any thing that depends on conditions.

Homeless people sleeping on benches along the sea wall.

If there must be pain, I accept it. The light within me rocks the tangle of selfishness to sleep.

Compulsively, for two days, hammering away at my story. What is this writing?

I house myself in a castle of affect. Gabilan aims to burst that bubble; I owe it to him and to everyone to burst it. To be like Fena, closer to the earth. Pure being—no pretense.

Shrieks of delight and applause in the street: the Christmas parade. The moon is full. I feel hungry and full at the same time.

An episode with the mirror. I look at myself.

"This is your face, this is your form. Be honest: can you forgive yourself?"

I know that the incongruities in my appearance are the deformities of my soul.

I go out walking. I am still unready.

I walk through the island made strange by the moon. I grow weary and sit on a curb, rubbing my eyes, under the huge fans of a sprawling Poinciana tree sifting the moonlight through its tiny lacy leaves. Tiny yards, palm trees, sea grapes, white wooden fences, lush foliage draped over everything. The debris of a parade in the street, revelers squealing.

I have not been living my beliefs. But what do I believe? What is the first thing I believe?

I look at my foot. It seems I have a body. Time is passing over me. I am getting older. This immature voice I use. It must fall off. But what am I? What am I to do?

There it is: fear. The mother holds the fear in her hand.

Spooky boutique houses. Eerie fallen leaves. Moonlight on streets with no horizon. I can't stay here! The mind is squirming.

Exile. Always the same story: this is not the place. Why is this not the place? What is "the place"?

Where am I now? I am passing a stained-glass window. The image of Christ on a cross. The window to the left is lit from the inside: a cross with a crown around its base.

I look again at the center window. It isn't Christ on a cross after all; it's risen Christ in a white robe. The spirit triumphant over death.

Isn't it death that is always rushing past, part of time, paring us? Paring away the contingency, until all that is left of us is God?

Breakfast at Denny's with Gabilan and Tula. Gabilan wants us all to work together on our story. Always coming up with ideas, collaborations.

The day is kind, though I lose awareness. I wake with anxieties. The problem is the one who says, "I might suffer!"

"What do I know?" Karla said. "I'm just an old woman!"
She cackled like a witch.

I am walking through a city, racks of clothing, plastic
tables. I see Inaru. He is burnt, he gives me a handful of ash.
I walk away in anger.

Paul's conversation comes back to me in bits and pieces.
His precise speech, holding me to a higher standard.

"There is never satisfaction, not even for an instant.
There is just this blessed unrest."

Morning sunlight in the back yard. Tula plays in the
leaves. Ana sits on the roof and smokes a joint. I read poems
by Li Po, leaning on the washing machine to catch the sun.
I walk Tula to Mallory Square. The sky is brilliant, pink. A
cruise ship moves like a huge creature in the water. Schooners
swoop by the pier. A unicyclist silhouetted against the sky.
A flame twirler.

My darling always comes when I am lovely as the moon.
I can't give him what I have prepared for him—he has no
pockets.

The Florida skies are full of migrations, the streets are
full of soldiers, empty of beggars, prostitutes, and thieves.

You can bet today there will be survival. That is not to
say there will be life.

My darling never comes when I am shabby, my
membranes tattered, my heart full of rust. Just holding his
book in my hand makes me happy. I don't have to read it.

I'm getting more permeable. To let things in, let things

out. To be on everybody's side, be everybody.

"It's time to get better," I whisper. But it seems my beloved hasn't heard, for he or I or all of us have locked him up again.

The nectar finds a space through which to flood, the trapped karmas find a space through which to flee: long ribbons of darkness and obscuration flow out. Don't I know that soon, all the world will be pure?

Ana brings me a long green skirt with bits of mirror sewn in. I can't muster hope.

"You are your own teacher," Paul says.

Such fanfare in my being, quite a show. Rippling, billowing. What could I do that might express what I feel, I ask at the end of a thunderous day. Overflowing with giving, but I can't find the world.

In the middle of the night, I wake and read in a pool of light, chin on one knee.

"At least when we were slaves we had food and shelter," the Israelites whine.

The wilderness: the cloud of unknowing, the dark night of the soul.

Inaru was in a holding cell for more than twenty-four hours. He read the Bhagavad Gita. I keep picturing him there, arrogant and spiteful, the book of ultimate truth open in his hand. Isn't he all of us?

What is this terrible fissure running through all of

humanity, this vein of guilt and shame which makes us suspect ourselves? The municipal cement, flecked with gum spots. The public trash cans, the cigarette butts, the rubber in which the trees are planted. My mediocrity, my cheaply-manufactured existence, my humdrum pathways, my callousness to exploitation.

A white light burning within me I go out seeking satisfaction. I am delirious, in the bar of fading embers, a hearth-fire playing on a flat-screen TV, a lake of red wine lilting in my glass, an erupting singer in a lace body-suit and fake eyelashes, taking the moments apart.

In drifts a man with wings. He has the most merciful smile, a mouth full of porous brown teeth. We talk of islands. We sit down in one another's hearts and swing our feet.

Ana comes, her eyes full of wax. I lose my body, becoming part of hers. We drift over streets without poignancy, the night redundant. Christmas lights wrapped around the palm trees, plastic ornaments falling out of both our mouths. Drunken infants in Schooner Wharf Bar. Retarded throngs of privileged persons, busy at their squandering. Black men work in the kitchen while white waitresses drift around like gazelles and giant children drool rivers of nickels and dimes into their aprons. This river of currency is transmuted into a heavy freight of products, the fruit of invisible labor. Ana returns to her boat; I walk, slightly broken-hearted, over the tourist strip.

Feebly, my mind cites the nuance. I enter a bar where people are playing amplified instruments. I dance like a flame, with a kind of flamingness I dance. People come to the flame to get warm—a woman with a reconstructed face sidles up to me. She whispers in my ear, "We are the cutest ones." I scowl at the band and lean on the wall, disgusted. I am out again, walking lonely on the street, asking, "Why have you forsaken me?"

The terrible thrashing panic with a gaping mouth. The need to feel safe, to be still. Placated, the panic becomes a mountain, a heart of peace with an ecosystem living upon her.

I write all morning on the roof.

Without my illusions, I am lost. I cast about.

Gabilan tells me about Don Quixote: "He looked in the mirror and he saw that he wasn't what he thought. He was just this crazy guy pretending to be a knight. He wanted to die, lost his will to live. He wanted to die, but all the other people who had been dreaming with him came to save him. 'If you die, we will die too,' they said. 'So you have to keep on dreaming!'"

Inaru cuts up a coconut and puts its milk and pulp into the food. I sit on the floor with Clarisse and ignore his interruptions as she relays her story. She has traveled, buried her father. She is a student of language, a poet. Inaru grows manic and slippery. He uses harsh words against a man delivering airport luggage to the house, accusing him of being racist.

"The revolution is stronger than ever," he says. He speculates about surveillance, about the motivations of the police. Yet he is childlike, taking apart the coconut husk, handing it to me to feel the cool freshness of the fibers.

We talk of existence, Clarisse and I seated on the floor, while Inaru cleans and Ana reclines, smiling softly, on the sofa. I explain the rift in the two schools of Zen, the story of the mirror: "The Southern school put less emphasis on ritual and formal meditation because the way they see it, we are already there."

As they leave together, I watch a coin landing plumb at the bottom of my heart—now I know how deep I am.

I am a child of many waters
and a child of others' dreams
my foremothers and forefathers
left the story incomplete
and they left a dying culture
from sea to shining sea
but I must accept what's offered
with utmost humility
with this begging bowl I wander
grateful for what I receive
nothing lost and nothing squandered
prophets sing like trembling reeds

I am a door to many wonders
that your eyes have never seen
I'm divided I am conquered
but I'm perfect underneath
so I have to take the tunnels
to discover what I mean
hear the Nyabinghi drummer
within every living being
deep down in the concrete jungle
ghetto moon, shine a beam
on the carnage of assumptions
otherness and color schemes
on immaculate seductions
by the feminine mystique
on the object and the subject
and the turf line in between
on the overcrowded gutter
on the unoccupied peak
on our spiritual corruption
like the Romans and the Greeks
our confusion like Columbus
never knowing where we reach

playing games of zero sum
with our mercenary fleets
yes in each and every one of us
the whole of them repeats
but day is done and gone the sun
now another light entreats
though our mother earth is smothered
and defiled, the moon is clean
as the night when the Taínos
slept upon the Caribbean
she illuminates the plunder
where it's sunken with a gleam
it was our haste that took us under
and our patience will redeem us
it was our slumber took us under
our awakeness will redeem us

I am a child of many waters
and a child of my own dreams
my foremothers and forefathers
changed history
and they left abundant harvests
for they planted many seeds
now Babylon's a garden
where we eat from all the trees
and they left a living spark
now the whole world catch a flame
it just takes united sharpness
and we break united chains

I'm a stone of many contours
that the builders could not place
now I hold the seat of honor
I'm the crown of all creation
I'm the half of every story
they never did relate

I'm the people's proper glory
humanity's true face
I'm a farmer, I'm an artisan
a martyr and a wailer
bush doctor, philosopher
the fruit of many failures
with the wisdom of the ancients
and an infant's spontaneity
manifested, one with nature
independent as a deity
and I do not have a border
for I do not serve a state
no periphery, no core
no security, no gate
no theater of war
no conflict on a stage
no jester in a court
no songbird in a cage
no double-edged sword
to cut the bittersweet cake
no chattel to import
on the whims of trade
no celestial shore
in heaven to await
nor one fine morning
when I'll fly away
over quandaries I'm soaring
boundaries I permeate
yes they found me in the storm
in the winds of change
yes they found me in the storm
yes I am the hurricane

11

There is a point where the possible meets the actual. Rest in there, it is guaranteed this far, no further. Immortal and invulnerable, this fragile moment exists.

The ways of thinking of the "others" have no roads into this open country. I am full of what I am. All the world is my heart, my beating heart, whose dreams are blood.

Such news is knocking at my doors, is pouring in my windows, traveling my roads. News of a single syllable that contains all language, lost language and unborn language. This moment may dissolve, and with it, this body of floss.

I am on both sides of existence, one foot in each river. The news comes from the other shore—pink magnolias in my ear. I have lived to fight another day.

I have seen the sorrows and fears, shards in a kaleidoscope, scarlet birds flocking back to their broken eggshells. All things as ecstasy and light, on a terrible journey, in a terrible disguise.

Sitting in the sunlight in the piano room, I try to think of a prayer, a hope, but I can't. I don't weigh anything in this body.

Our grandfathers are dust in the wind, bones in the cold, cold ground. Our grandmothers are growing transparent, ethereal, slipping out of their dresses of reflected light.

Many days pass, far from the waters of words, untouched the path, overgrown the path. Fears and negations crowd around the new art.

A meeting between the universal self and the match-stick self. Not only does this little twig of carbon journey toward the white light, but the white light is also on a journey, a long blue journey toward a tiny carbon heart. Perhaps the light will meet the ash half-way.

I am afraid of failing, of what the others think. When will I remember that behind their masks, it is my own soul that looks on?

"I'm still alive," I say.

Inaru has fallen from the sapodilla tree and broken a vertebra. He talks as if his jaw is clenched.

Nick irons his shirt, talking of choices. Lucy tidies the room, moving slowly her long puppet arms.

Green-eyed Nick, speaking from the bottom of a well. I cannot speak this language, not with my eyes, not with my hands. This language flows beneath us, without our help.

"I want to be the man that's perfect for her."

"Just shells," I say. "Just whistling shells."

Lucy moves her hands in the hot tub, playing with the foam. She is like an angel, soft and barely real.

The stream of being coming through me, falling into patterns—the obstacle is in the stream of being. I wrap around my thoughts; I am the space around the thoughts, the place where the thoughts meet the space. Is there such a place? Everywhere and no particular place.

Lucy kneels beside me on the carpet and touches my back.

I am made of good things. I am food.

Snow on the rooftops, my tragedy quiet and at-home.

Bare trees flowing by outside. I blink slowly, knowing "I am sad".

Lucy buys me a pair of earrings in the winery gift shop.

Whenever Lucy leaves the room, Nick asks where she has gone. Lucy in the cherry blossoms, unable to save us.

"There's no money in agriculture," Nick says. A glint of silver tragedy in his eye.

"We are all a bit squandered," Arjun says.

We can't be human without other humans. The world will not be saved by grand gestures. It will only be saved by small, ordinary gestures between small, ordinary beings.

I am banishment, "the way the chips fall." Swaths of fog roam the slopes of the blue mountains. Foreigners mingle with locals in a forced way. I hang on the edges of conversations. I smile empty smiles, haunt the outskirts of authenticity. The women's eyes cut sideways. Their laughter is frantic, their comments bizarrely-timed.

Outside, I look for a place to weep. My eyes linger on the bamboo fence, the papaya trees. When I pick up a thread of this color, the other threads like this rise, too. This wasteland straddles oceans, crosses borders in a single step, pulls mountain-tops down and lifts valleys up. It covers the entire map.

Youth melts off like a flower dying in my lap.

"How will you live your dreams now," Suicide asks, "marked as you are by age?"

Night comes, the warmth vanishes. I stand near the fire,

consumed from within. The party crackles and murmurs. I drown in my own darkness. No one extends me a branch—their boats, anyway, are full of holes.

A huge palm bathed in moonlight opens into the sky: an explosion of tropical being, fed on the blood of the sea winds. Violence hisses through the foliage. I am a battleground. Now that the victims have been carried away, the field lies lonesome, pock-marked and indifferent.

What am I holding onto in these silences and postures? Why do I not carry myself on my own two feet, away from this illusory city of in and out?

I am hungry, and Shamar gives me food. Noticing I am cold, he offers me a sweater. I am alone. He invites me to walk with him the paths. I have forgotten who I am. He tells me, "You're not like the others."

He says, "I can take you places. You won't want to go back."

He tries to pull me up the rocks, then through some careless gesture casts me out of the charmed circle.

"What do you know about suffering?" Ras Ptah asks me. "Have you lived outside for one year? With no mother or father to give you food when you're hungry? With no pillow, no blanket, your bones cold? No friend to talk to, dirty? Then tell me: what do you know about suffering? You're on one side, and I'm on the other. I'm on the side where anything can happen to me."

"The Buddha was a king," Ras Ptah explains, "and he lived in the palace. One day, he started to wonder what it was like outside the palace. They said that if he left, he could never come back. He left anyway.

"Outside the palace, he saw a farmer tilling the soil. The farmer uncovered a worm. A bird suddenly flew down and ate the worm. So the Buddha saw the uncertainty of life.

"Buddha said the body is an aggregate of suffering; because we strive for satisfaction, we suffer. So he tried to remove from people this unnecessary burden. He walked with a begging bowl. If night fell while he was on the road, he slept there. If a storm came, he went through the storm. He just wore a little robe."

Downtown, an infinite calamity is progressing. A man is writhing on the ground, his clothes the same dusty color as his skin. The teenage boys take no notice of him, presiding over headless wire mannequins arrayed in nylon and polyester. Women stand in the sun among piles of clothes, their arms weighed down by wire hangers, eyes roving desperately over the faces of passersby.

At the bay, men hold coiled fishing line in their hands. The surging water swirls with cheap artifacts, offering the city back its exquisite debris. A stingray surfaces now and then among the styrofoam. Expanses of city grid lie silent, undisturbed by a single footfall, roamed by flocks of plastic.

Hand-painted advertisements blush with shame, pinned naked above their evacuated empire. A pigeon is dead beside a traffic light, its eyes open, looking at the sky. I stumble upon a grave fitted in among the sidewalk slabs.

In a leafy yard, a group of musicians are playing. The crowd moves in ecstasy. A man dressed in white jerks his body in a natural, un-stylized dance. He shakes his head, shouts. A woman, her eyes and cheeks sunburned, breaks into song. Individual selves swirl like the city trash on this seamless, primordial current.

We sit on the benches just inside the gate. Potted plants and sculptures have accumulated: a giant Tiki man, his penis broken off and placed in his mouth. A skeleton riding a bicycle, suspended in the mango tree.

The crushed leaves that carpet the ground between the houses, the climbing vines that cling to the shed. I sleep nestled between two canoes among leaves and twigs on the tin roof.

Light spills from Nina's window onto the tiny porch. Wind chimes tinkle; the streets are quiet. This soft ease orchestrated by so much misery not far across the sea. I find my dresses in the box on the roof. Inaru cuts cabbage over the pot, pours milk from a hairy brown coconut.

The old men in the market stands on Duval Street, caught in their daily round, growing feeble and spotted. Mark doing the crossword, sneaking a spliff. Joe dizzy and clouded. Their neuroses splinter and multiply. The conversation replays, growing more absurd. The tourists drifting by implode, self-destruct, nothing to combat except their own membranes.

Old mysteries being solved, and my being resolved, dissolved. How much is circumstance, how much is soul?

Is the soul separate from circumstances? Does it move in a line, like a ribbon, or a cloud of dust?

I sleep with a Bible for a pillow. A pair of golden eyes illuminates the snaking tree branches. We invite death into our being. The sadness, the chagrin at the wreckage and despondency of our lives, seen through the eyes of God.

Americans move about in vacation clothes, in soft bodies, soft lives. Black maids slip between the houses. Heavy undulations in my spirit. God feels around in my humanity: thick like molasses, like lava. There is a fallacy in it.

Even when performing only for oneself, there is still an imputed audience, a court of justice, a tape running. The days pass like dreams, without leaving a mark. Waking in the sunshine and leaves. All night I felt far from my meaning, envious of those who have found their work. Then comes the knowing: everything is in its place. It shall all be necessary.

Ras Ptah: "Do what has never been done before. Help whom has never been helped before."

God looks on the humans, busy destroying the miracle. Day after day they tear it down, calling it necessity. They believe they have to clip their wings. In the softness of American life, the hardness of other places is hidden. The artificial world, soft and planed and antiseptic, full of dreamlike products smooth as clouds.

Love arrives and envelops form, in this place where the world meets the skin. In the nostrils, in the helixes, the torn links, the spaces, the places where being is matter, between the life that is dead—inert, static as a tombstone, the free unlimited spirit, crystallized.

I reach for my pen, I add to a rhyme.

Imbalance, the mind burning like a torch, a consuming fire—distracting, making a theater of the quiet swamps.

A reel of candy streets and trolley tours spinning through the days.

Beside the water Inaru laughs, shaking down to his roots. It is God laughing. I thread my adoration into the edges of his being. I have long since let go.

An ache in the world, something dragging us down. Death has come again among me. I ask Gabilan while I'm painting the door, "Don't you fear death?"

"There's nothing I can do about it," he says. "But I try to make the best of what I have. Which is more than you can say."

Samantha and I take the baby to the beach. She chases gulls on the coral that tinkles like glass underfoot.

Inaru's grandmother touches me when she speaks.

An emptiness about me, an emptiness I have created.

Sweetness and depth. Being born. Scraps of cloud drifting. Enchantment in the trees. A gliding hawk, the feathery Poinciana boughs. The music touching the deep threads of my soul.

I don't remember what I aimed to say. The day has worn on, lost its fresh dreams. I don't belong to them anymore.

The moon is waning, soft and tropical. Rain whispering in the night.

Passion like a fire leaves the landscape wasted. The

ego throws nets into empty waters. Rage ripples through me, creasing the sands. You can see it in the faces of the people—the gore and devastation reflected in the sides of great waves. The heavy foot of futility lying over my dreams.

Putting the child-self to sleep. I hold her in my arms, watch her fade and disappear. I rock her to death. We weep together at the death of our child. We close her eyes.

I touch the broken heart of my child. The wounds are old, so very old. I am the only one who can heal them. The problem is not you, I tell the wounded child. The problem is in the mind of the people.

I wake to worship the world. Such stories the leaves are telling. They nuzzle, embrace.

What choice am I to make?

"If you pay attention to what you really need," Nina says, "you are everything you need. It's all around you."

It's bigger than me, so I must get out of the way. I am with the obstacle now; my heroism is on trial. Will I be buried, or will I fight my way to freedom, to life? Buried in an ant-hill like Valmiki. I feel the anger of colonization, reflected fire, sickness.

The wastes of my youth, the inertia. Can I believe in my own timelessness, can I tune myself to eons? Perhaps the seeds I believed lost and squandered will yet emerge. Perhaps those heavy steps through sunken valleys can be redeemed.

The love you are not ready to give today, perhaps tomorrow you will give. The tragedies of the past are not dead and gone. They are here and now, and we go on healing them for all time.

For days, I wake with the feeling "I am bad." Guilt and shame. The Poinciana boughs are turning orange in the heat. The rain seems to implicate me. Yet a new hope is with me. I talk with Olive of our ancestors.

I sit, paralyzed by opposing notions. In my dream, there were notions, each one living in its house. "Balance, balance," some voice said. "Do not live in any house but know who is living in each house." Each statement was made by one of the houses, and it could only be decoded by the way it was affected by the gravity of the other houses. They completed one another's language.

"I'm not getting any younger," Samantha says. We watch the sun go down on a blanket in the sharp weeds. The sky is too wonderful, we cannot comprehend it in our misery.

The whole of time is a body. The moments of the past are bones, linked to the bones of the present. The present does not go anywhere without the past. It must all be resolved. The work is immense. Everyone is coming, not one being can be left behind. We are one another's bodies. It is literally true.

Water festival is beginning in Nupo. The monks grow stern and immobile, ready to wait. At night the frogs roar and thunder.

We waited weeks for the first rains. We grew hot, dazed. A drizzle woke me in the morning. It turned to a rushing white deluge, cleaning the tin roof, washing the streets and trees.

I saw my mind as a cloud, the clouds drifting over the mind, all the clouds going in one direction. Swirling clouds blowing, and around my belly a motionless horizon.

I saw the people becoming happy. I became very heavy, and I pulled at the love through my big roots. My ancestors were watching me.

In the center of the big fat trunk of the tree, there was becoming, change happening. The old self was transmuted, giving way to the new self. A crucifixion was going on, a passion. The branches, exuberant, called birds to live in them, talking to the sun about ecstasies.

Then—momentum. A leaning, a motion. I pulled up the sails, let the wind go by, became perpendicular. I saw Inaru and Clarisse: their wonderful spirits, their power. I vowed to give to either of them whatever boon they may ask. I saw their daughter, a powerful baby girl.

My heart grew crowded, overcome, tight. The birds began to sing with virtuosity, after the rain. The mangoes are ripening, growing heavy on the branches. Two years have passed.

Seeing through things, deep seeing. The body as if holding on to death, keeping death nearby, a trap door. Darkness, despair and discomfort: sharp tools, good for cutting.

Then Inaru passes, giddy, with the news. It is true there will be a child.

A deity comes and sits in me, a Peter Pan. The ache that this old Wendy body feels for the Peter Pan spirit that has flown in through her windows.

"I want" like headlights piercing the darkness.

On one hand, a bloody sunset. On the other, a full moon rising.

I invite the pain inside, an honored guest.

I barely look at the horizon any more. I'm watching the drunks beneath the coconut trees.

Today I'm sitting in my skin
but one fine morning I'll move on

that's why I always aim my darts
at the great beyond

the fireflies may waltz all night
and not produce ID

the woods just trusts they'll do what's right
and die in the first freeze

he's playing for eternity,
the fiddler on the street

pedestrians stop their hourglasses,
let their sands blow free

the truth is an explosion
you and I we are the flames

both root and rainbow move in us
and answer to our names

and if you feel divided
as if pierced by cutting blades

that's a sign you're solid
and you're standing in the way

your true self is a whittler
of immaculate designs

you shed all but the thinnest thread
and pass through the third I

you love just like the deep blue sky
your lovers' hearts don't break

but enter into vastness
and wind up wide awake

12

I stand in a cloudy dawn at the roots of the live oak trees. Sal's blue eyes look past me. He is smaller, his beard and hair shorter, as if he has grown more distant, or younger, like Merlyn. The sun has left kisses on his cheekbones. His melting eyes are clean. His gnarled hands work the gears and wheel of the truck.

I see the world from beyond my life—the strange circumstances, the dizzying quandaries. I am willing to know how I can help.

Birds in the cypresses. Wide streets. The smell of oak leaves in the silty soil. Childhood memories. Time, as difficult to catch as rain.

Even these thoughts are like the wild frost patterns, the roads rain takes across glass, the random fruit of forces meeting. Everything is 'it.' The miracle: I am in it.

The air in the room is a being, the long fall of light. The voices of the birds. Ordinary mind, too, is a being with a life.

There is room, but there is only room because of death. We crouch too much over our egos, our tickers. Prayer as dance, as love. Growing like trees toward the sun. Dealing in dark currents. A river runs down my brain.

"I haven't accomplished anything," I tell Amar. The bald, empty city frightens me. I doubt everything. A voice says, "I'm sad." I listen to the voice.

I see the people I know, each reflecting light differently.

Laura shimmering at an angle. I feel her warmth. I feel how she is an extension of my body. The chasm of her lack. You try to pour her a gift, but she pushes it away.

Sandiman with an unbroken gaze. In his eyes there is stillness, respect.

"I want to know what I'm working toward," I say.

"You don't have to work toward anything. Why do you have to have a goal? I am just doing the same thing. I sleep a lot, so I can dream. I came here three years ago with nothing, selling my pieces on the ground. Now I have everything—a house, a car. I want to get rid of it all and do something new."

We walk toward the river. My mind is askew. The old houses and old streets. Not here, says my mind.

The French Quarter, cluttered with the relics of a stupid and painful past. The buildings crawl with history's stifled cries. A razor wire of privilege cuts through the richest of possibilities, sparing only the Fat Man and his handful of wind. You can see him on every corner, his costume grown so thin that every tourist and painted clown notices his naked greed.

Even the river wants to turn her head. She writhes in her bed, lurching for the shorter, swifter route, the Atchafalaya. Hoards of tiny men keep her locked in her archaic and fabulous tracks, pushing her cheek up against Decatur Street, holding her still while she makes the Fat Man rich.

"I don't feel well," I say.

Sandiman watches with fascination as the train passes. He looks at everything, opened up all around.

"I'm afraid," I say.

"You get scared too easily."

His living eyes are turned to the living river. He stands, statuesque in the clouds. A drunk man tells us the police won't let him carry his sword. His grandfather was Jean Lafitte, did we know that? Sandiman just looks at him, then breaks a smile, breathes a laugh. Daisies ruffle in the breeze. Sandiman is looking at the water, not thinking about the water.

The fountain of consciousness. Two ends of one stick. Looking under stones in the mind.

"Teach and learn," Amar says. "Poetry is your weapon. The pen is the sword."

I read him his poem. He knows when it's over. "Beautiful," he says. "I'm blushing."

His face is like a cloudy sky.

Letting myself become fluid. Cutting cords, shedding weights. "Make your home in the wind."

Negation. Regret, a purple, inky weight, descending from the right side. Guilt on one side, and pride on the other side. When pride is inverted, there is guilt.

The Concrete Waves is a garden now.

Amar: "I am the Louisiana welcoming committee. I want to cook for you." He brings food for us wretches.

At the typewriter I feel calm. The same things that give us relief cause us pain. I look at my being. I am not what I thought. Such pathos. It's so sincere, devastatingly sincere. Everything is finished, but nothing is finished.

Come down, Indra urges Brahma. Yes, we will go down. Fearless now, less squeezed and panicky. Charmed by the city sights. Charmed, as snakes are charmed. Brush strokes of powerlessness. Pearls of doom. I long for someone I have never met. Knives in my head, and I am left bleeding. The trees drip like jewels.

Sometime during the rainstorm, my misery ended. Amar plays the santur. Someone on piano, another on sax. Every heart in the place is wounded: so many smaller wounds gathered around this bigger wound. The prison is my own mind. These generous clouds, diamond rains, rainbow rains. I pray to be love in the morning, but I don't remember to be love until blue night-fall.

"All this love falls in," Victor says. "It's everywhere, it's just pouring into me."

One man shines his car, the other holds a sign under the bridge. With the dark weight of old certainty on my lap, new possibilities fly like birds around my head. The sky is already realized, is already everything it wanted to be. Are the pigeons on the chimneys the same pigeons or different from the pigeons of the past? We are not the same, not different, they say. Same and different are your ideas.

Footprints made of sky. Rouses, wearing a mask of reflected evening. The street pauses to listen to the opera singer. A man leans on his umbrella. Everyone wears their secret smiles. My darkness has been visiting me. The cement evaporates from the brick chimney like a cloud. The sky turns to honey. After all the destruction and madness, New Orleans goes on selling chandeliers. There is a bird singing in the blue street.

Rosa's, shipwrecked, stormy.

Amar: "It's like you see a cute cat and you say, 'Oh, how beautiful,' but you don't want to take it home. We should take responsibility. Everyone should take responsibility."

On the Industrial Canal, high grass leans and lolls in a hot wind. The Claiborne Bridge sweats traffic. A tugboat is tied against the wharf, ready to slide between the lush thighs of the coast. A fish's jaw lies bare upon the levee, the flesh eaten clean by flies.

I walk among the weeds of forsaken dwellings while the giants of steel and concrete bear away their daily bread. My mind is a white bell, sweet with nectar: an angel's trumpet gleaming among the chaos and destruction of the riverbank.

The landscape has been ravaged in the name of this strange flower. Infatuated with its rare powers, they place sacrifices upon its altar, the pyres of air-conditioning, packaged foods, deep, cold refrigerators. A new world is conjured to house this whimsical and delicate bud. Yet the primordial ooze seeps in, licking the soft petals of the mind with flame. Every flower is stained with the footprints of death, and finally gives itself to shadow. What end then could ever justify such means?

"The greatest aspiration is to empty samsara completely. That is your real purpose."

Sitting with Peter, facing his paintings on Jackson Square.

"Are there days when you don't sell anything?"

"Oh, yeah. We're coming up on three or four of them now."

I suddenly know how much is at stake. The abyss is all around. All that stands between existence and oblivion is me. This is it—there is no other moment.

"You have never looked under your thoughts, under phenomena, to see what is really going on," the lama says.

Talking to death, using another language. Memories of long time in that suburban world. Unreconciled memories flood in.

In the street at night Zero says, "Everything seems so real to me these days." I notice again the trees, clouds, power lines.

"It's not that one day it will all make sense," Zero says. "It's about being, right now. Just pay attention to the person you're becoming, moment by moment."

In the darkroom I feel a kind of peace. The trees at the back of the park: mystical, alive.

"It's existence you're the victim of," the mind says. "Everything, just by existing, creates imbalance. So easy to place blame—the world simply mismanages itself."

My own brilliance, my own true light, so bright it cancels out everything that is "me." My own light is the remedy for "me." Light melts the demons who have been running things—they dissolve into love. The spheres align, a smile appears on my face. My light goes out in glints, in waves, so that the core of existence, the heart itself is brilliant with clarity.

There is obscurity in the clarity? Transcendence needs something to transcend? Fogs in me, death-fogs. Not-here, some humans say. We are the world, and we will pull our own destruction down on ourselves.

The clouds are piled high, wetting the moon. A brass band strikes up. Train song showers flowers on our tombs.

Changes in my form. I feel alien to myself. What am I for?

Amar: "When you cry, that is the shine. Like a jewel, when the light hits it, it shines. When you cry, that is your shine."

I see Roberto. His deep, genuine source remains unchanged.

Rae: "Don't break my heart. See what I see."

What am I hoping for?

Amar: "You have to try harder. You have to create your language."

Sunday night, June about to end, the ceiling fans hover like dragon-flies inside the Praline Connection, dreams without a dreamer.

The atmosphere has begun to drink me, the air is drinking from my skin. The love between me and the cypresses, the oaks so tragic, their arms falling in all directions like shrapnel, like hearts broken open. I think of the distant places.

"I have no right to be lost," something says.

Zero, and the slow motion of the summer. The quiet of it, its humility. Maddening, grief-stricken love. The sleeping doorway of Cafe Brazil. The place growing through me, the place free of questions in one's heart.

"Let yourself change. Let yourself change." I stop recreating a world wherein there is a problem. I remember the nothingness that is the backdrop of life—clinging becomes absurd. Time will sweep it all away; the only response is astonishment.

The sky humid, purple, rolling. The sky is alive, speaking to me. The sky and I are in relationship, our souls touching. There are seeds falling on me, extending through me. I am held here, heavily held.

The women waxed and painted are nearer to the money-god—to them doors are opened. The women burnt and bulging are cursed by the money-god. People leave space around them, fearing the pull of their wake.

The spirit is very close—it is right here.

"I am here," God says. "What is your question?"

There is no question.

If I am quiet enough, I can see the currents flowing.

The only way to be clean is to stop clinging to dirt. Cleaning my spirit, all the way down to the roots—and beyond, into the soil.

I open the door to lack and loss, to heartbreak. Come in. In come the lack, the loss, the heartbreak: a sooty breath, swirling, filling the room, closing the eyes, choking the lungs.

There isn't much world left; the souls have already begun departing. Will I be left behind? The shadow is so great, so red and heavy I can't leave it. I am frozen, in over my head, suffering, beyond hope. There is only stoicism left, bracing oneself in the tremendous wind. There is only pulling in one's arms and legs, waiting for things to be different.

What am I being punished for? For seeking praise in the wrong place—on the outside. For relying on the paper money of the empire. For clinging to things that are slippery.

The sound of Percy's crutches clopping up the block. Amar feeds us, asking nothing in return.

"I can see my name in big sign. Amar's Kebab, and ice from heaven." The lights change on the block, red and green diffusing into the wet air, lacing themselves into the leaves around the patio, the cement slabs rising over the roots of the tall sycamore tree. A mournful ballad slides down the walls.

Amar says again to get back in the fight. The clouds very low and wet. The street out of tune, in shambles. The regular drunks on crates outside the old A&P. Spurts of indecisive sunlight. Under the bridge, a woman motions with her hand to her mouth. The moon is still hiding.

The clouds are tall as flutes. The crickets are praying, cicadas are praying, the airplane is praying, and I. I hear the world breathing. I open all the doors—the devils come and go as they please.

While I was speaking with Zero, the houses were sliding back and forth in the mud. They got closer to listen in and then receded and began to sneak off—they tilted off the horizon. The power lines and the skin of the road melted away. I noticed that Zero and I were nothing but drawings in the clay of the earth.

Frenchmen Street is sooty in its darkness. The eyes have their shutters unlocked and they are rattling. Zero and I sit by the river.

Zero says, "There are thousands of points of colors in the infinite distance." The clouds come very close to us. Everything is alive: the sky, the lights. I watch the lights shaking down the skirts of the river.

The wharf, a red glow at the Dragon's Den. They are howling hymns in the Spotted Cat. Zero is singing. He lies on the river walk and laughs. He tells a story about the river being a man turned black by the oil of the river boats.

The sky cleared, three stars could be seen. Zero sang: "Life was so, until she, until she."

Even time is alive. Shedding fears—I am free of this guilt. I have done it, I have done what I came to do. The place was already beloved. Then there was someone else in it. The lake was vocal, almost roaring. Sadness like a canopy over the mind.

"What is the sadness like?" Zero asks.

"It's hot like anger, but it's talking to fear."

Zero speaks in pictures: "After living on the mountain, I finally came down and looked in the mirror. There was this light swirling in my eyes. 'You are so beautiful,' I said."

"There is a voice that talks to me sometimes. But it only talks once in a while, and it talks in puffs."

"My armor all came off and I saw that I was made of glass. My heart exploded. It was almost like heartbreak, but it wasn't—it was the truth. It was beautiful to see. But then people just wanted to suck it dry and break it."

Amar's eyes are large and round, the spaciousness of spirit, ether. His suffering is written on his face. He tells us, sitting in the darkened cafe, how he used to save every insect from the water trough. One by one he would rescue each ant, each bee, each cockroach.

"It took me thirty minutes, before school every day. But for them, it was like an ocean. Imagine if you were drowning in an ocean and a boat came and saved you."

The first mask he made, after his daughter died: "I was trying to get something out, and I didn't know what it was. I made all kinds of things, snakes and alligators, I had to fold the clay and fold it again. Finally, I made it, a woman's face, coming out of these layers of tough skin, like alligators, snakes. It was something I saw in Rosa's face, and in my daughter's, and in my mother's too; it was all women in the world. The tough skin because they have survived it all, all the struggling and bullshit of the earth, yet even delicate and small they have stayed.

"When I got it, then I knew, and I could finally rest. I made it for people who were dying, people who got it. I never wanted to sell it. I was listening to a lot of music in those days. Leonard Cohen. I was so depressed. I couldn't even move. My friends tried to get me out of it, but I took a long way. It was a beautiful journey. I gained so much from it. Being happy and partying is fine, but you don't really gain anything that way."

A saxophone player goes wild on the corner, shouting, stomping, bringing us things from his layers. I have seen him before. What is it blows him around the world, chases him from corner to corner? His brilliance is too bright—it dances on his gestures and crackles around his feet. Lightning paints cloudscapes; the rain returns, the genius retreats, like one who has been scratching at the dust.

"You see those people," Amar says, "so talented, so much feeling. But they don't get what they deserve, and they never ask for it. They end up on Frenchmen, playing for people who just pass them by. Soon they have a missing tooth here and there, their beard is growing. They still play with feeling, but they never get what they deserve, and they never ask."

A drunken man comes along, looking desolate, rigid with a cry he wants to unleash.

"How are you," I ask.

He shrugs, as if to shake me off the face of his suffering.

"I lost a wife and sister and daughter three years old and mother-in-law to a drunk driver who killed them and burned them. I loved them all. She worked for the IRS; I worked on the road for the coal company. I married late, after Vietnam. I got four purple hearts."

He wanders off, still mumbling.

Roy sits on a stool, drapes it in pink cloth. He sits on the box, his brass jar before him, pedestrians drifting indifferently all around. He plays the first notes, frantic and plaintive clarinet notes resounding in the corridor of the street. We are not worthy of his gift.

Zero says, "I woke up in the morning and everyone was afraid. I went to work, and everyone was afraid. I passed through the city and everyone was afraid. I went back home, and everyone was afraid."

The dark spirit he knew as a child: "The sound stretched out through my infinite subconscious. The sound of a pin dropping in a silent, empty street. I was the sound."

His dream: "I went toward the light, but then I became the light. There was fire in the water. Water and fire were one without destroying each other."

Amar says, "Your hero is bleeding. And you have the medicine." His face is like a burning field.

"I want to write a book about you," I say. "A book with soft pages."

A gallery of woe, crying from the back, lower realm.

You will never know, something says.

Never know what?

Whether you are valid, whether you exist. You will never see yourself exist.

In the mud, in the deep roots, there is no horror of existing, no fear of being. There is no border there. Infinite chain of being, infinite embrace in every direction. Freedom in the knowledge that even if it is through defeat, through breakdown, I will be released. What must emerge will emerge—God, the truth.

The clown is passed out on the sidewalk. The girl from the souvenir shop checks him for life, kisses him on the cheek, and walks on.

A girl holds a sign, facing the stopped cars, pointing

the way to our doom. The prophets and the pipers gather dollars from the waves, the waves of tourists.

A woman, softly intoxicated, descends from the curb and filters between the parked cars. Money has made things possible, and she moves in that realm of possibility, her measure of sovereignty rippling all around her. There is pain here, but the pain doesn't hurt me. My sovereignty is too thick to penetrate. Where does the pain go when it goes rippling down my impossible skin? What does it become when it does not become hurting?

"I'm glad to hear," Amar says. "I want to put it in my ear. It made me shed tear. I'm taking medicine so I can get cure."

"Better to stay pure. Like you always were before. Good sir."

"I'm glad you're nea-ur."

"That doesn't rhyme!"

"Yes, it does. It's very clea-ur. I'm glad you're losing your fea-ur."

The days pass, untouched, birds playing in the sky. A smattering of people outside Rouses, the washboard, the fiddle, a couple dancing in the middle of the street. The chandeliers are twinkling, the pedicab driver is paused, a father bouncing a blond-haired baby in the seat of the carriage. An old drunk man smiles and dances, directing traffic. The musicians bored and ravishing against the dusty-pink wall, cigarettes lolling from their mouths, bathed in lemon-water street lamps and the glow from the window of the souvenir shop. A breeze lifts my hair, moves a lady's long skirt. Zero bikes into a blood red sunset.

Fulfillment comes from within. There is a wound in the world, and I am the space there, made of wishes and boons.

"Be true to yourself, or everything you do will go wrong," says the master.

I am experiencing soreness, the past. Comparing myself with others. Dissonance between thought and reality.

"It will hurt," says the master. "You will be devastated. But don't let it stop you. It's coming out."

I put distance between myself and my happiness.

The moon is looking me in the eye. I find poverty, lack. Rain on Royal Street. The sky is so loud the stars cannot be heard. Everything crackling and dirty. I have stepped back into the shadow. Rings and baubles in the long puddle along the curb.

My spirit is wailing. My eyes are hot, the air is still.

I rest as if I have accomplished something remarkable. Actually, I barely know myself. Living in a cloud, in a world without an earth. The sky swirls in Rae's high windows. I stay home all day while a storm brews in the distance. I have a silence with me that can only be broken by a great fall.

All is lost. This is my own apocalypse, and it contains infinite possibilities.

Zero smoothed the lines of my face with his fingers. In one eye I looked different from how I looked in the other eye. We walked beyond the wall I had never crossed before, and there was the Florida Street bridge. The pink light was spilling over the levee. At Rosa's, the leaves were wet with light. The radio played over the speakers, tucked in among the Christmas lights. People were smiling on the corner.

Let things organize themselves. I was lost for a day, up against dead ends. Roy and I for a moment share gladness of each other, his smile in his tattooed face as he holds onto the pole. I lug things through the park, but there is a dead body and the police officer wouldn't let me pass. Death, closure, dead ends. The night another dead end.

Zero comes with me to the lake.

"Look at the light!" he keeps saying. The sunset is orange in the leaves of the oaks, but I can't see anything. I can see that I myself am the monolith, heavily entrenched in my habit.

The city goes dark. The hopes I have been building on begin to shift. Under the sweetness, a fearsome mask leers. The world is haunted by wounds and hungers. I become a wasteland.

I go to the river, but the river cannot cool the fire in my mind.

Zero says, "When your cup is empty, I will fill it. And when my cup is empty, you can fill mine. For no reason at all."

The street climbing with vines, ceiling fans and big trees. I lie in the hammock while Zero plays the guitar.

"I'm in my boat," I say.

He blows across me, pretending to be the sea breeze. The child glowing in his eyes, in his big smile, where he is still a baby.

"You can throw a rock at something," Zero says, "or you can push a boulder onto it."

In Zero's eyes, the smooth, round edges of faith, the perfectly round circumference of eternity. Every loose end tied, every frayed edge mended, every stray doubt seen in its wholeness, absorbed by its origin and destination. He nods, blinking slowly. He is looking at the river, singing. I notice: he is praying.

"Love is light," he says. "It cannot be destroyed. Even if a light shines into a vast darkness and is dissipated, it's still light. Love is the same way. If you love something and you just keep loving it, the thing you love will start to reflect that. Whether you're growing a plant or loving a person, it always works."

"Why are the people so broken?"

"They're shattered, and drugs are like glue—they make them feel put back together. But the only thing that can really put them back together is love."

A wounded bird, a bird pretending to be wounded, to distract us from her babies. Three Thai monks in the street. "Sawat dee kha," I say, and press my hands together. They are surprised and delighted.

The world goes on, the empire evacuated, Armstrong Park full of drifting air and silence. There are no more places; everyone is leaving. There is no one to talk to, there is no theater, no show. Everyone is an extension of the self.

Nothing is happening.

I become everything at once; this is what it means to die. My thoughts taper off into the spectrum, wrapped up all around in their opposites.

Amar: "When you take a step in the journey of love, be careful. What looks like a flower might be a snake. What looks like water might be poison. Keep going! Don't drink! Keep going until you are so thirsty you think you can go no further. Go further still. Then you will witness a miracle: your heart becomes an ocean."

Laura: "We can't know what will happen. That's the art of the world. All these random factors coming together and creating something—it could be anything."

Within that infinite possibility, carnage, spilled blood. That too.

Zero says, "It's like going down a hill with your brakes on. You waste all the energy that would carry you back up the hill. It's better to just let go."

"Instead of pushing," he says later, "Don't. Set your compass, but you can't go any faster than the current."

The big heavy armored people lumping around, crushing the crystal people. Love spills out of the crystal people and runs down the streets and gutters.

The miracle of the heart, trampled-upon, ignored. The miracle of the heart which doesn't remember that it is a miracle, thinks it is worthless and acts worthless, putting on a smile when it wants to bum a cigarette, holding out a plastic cup while the tourists pass by like glittering boats.

Zero says, "You can't know someone else's journey, but it's the heart where people are connected. The heart can express itself to satisfaction, but the mind never can. The heart can laugh and then relax. But if the mind laughed all day, as soon as it stopped laughing it would think another thought."

Waveland. A rainstorm. Flocks of birds roaming through a dangerous sky, the shoals concealing slicks of stolen fire. Zero wades out into the water. It isn't until later that I realize the storm was my own.

"Thoughts are like rivers—they carry you on journeys, sometimes simple and direct on their way to the truth, sometimes long and winding, with wizards and donkeys. But they always have to go back to the source.

"In the Amazon, they say there is one father sun in the center of the universe and all the other light and life flows from there. The chance of being born in this body is the same as a turtle coming up for air in a certain floating ring in the middle of the ocean. When I heard that, I thought at first about how lucky I was. But then it occurred to me that I had been trapped."

"When you love something, it changes," Thomas Merton writes.

This work evaporates into the ether, slides away, down the seams of the world, escapes with the carnival of clouds, returns to the source. Zero is there, already there. He waters the plants. No one has yet told him that he is what they are all looking for, that he is what they really need.

Look inside any phenomenon and you will see the glittering light of mind. The season is changing, the moon is new. It is my fear that says, "Not here." It remembers being trapped in other autumns.

The panic—Zero says, "The power in rootedness is that you can weather any storm. You just can't be moved."

Laura weeps beside the lake. There are storms on the horizon.

The sky is flushed with bands of pink after the rain.

"You're not alone," Zero says.

I watch the rainstorm ripple over the lake, the whole world white with death. Zero speaks about the men who raised him, the cruelty they inflicted on women, children and animals.

"Just so they could exist. Just so they could feel like they were real on this plane."

I pour myself into a mold, preparing for a professional world. Zero remains at the mouth of the fountain, undressing his spirit.

"The system" only lets us grow one way, like trees whose possibility it prunes. So much has been lost to this.

Money cannot affect the limitless truth, the eternal life of all beings, including those mowed down by the blades of capitalism, patriarchy, utilitarianism.

"I forgive you," I chant. "I forgive you, I forgive you."

I forgive everything, time itself. Tragedies on all sides I forgive; the jagged edge of reality.

Dissonance, the new which is not yet touched by language.

"I keep getting the blues," Zero says. "The distance the wind has to travel over the face of the planet. The vastness of time. How slowly time moves."

We sit beside the levee.

"If God were a heroin addict, New Orleans would be the rubber band he put around his arm to find his vein. Then he fell asleep and forgot to take it off."

The bayou is very still, reflecting houses across the street. A fish jumps from the water.

People dressed in ideas rather than materials. Two homeless men share the contents of a styrofoam box. The pigeons reign, playing with their own sharp shadows on the asphalt. Then it is as if a hand had stirred us. People of all colors push by, known well by the sun. The cloud above has broken into a new shape, sharp and like a key. Where it is going, my heart longs for that place. Then it is gone.

A flock of tourists rolls by. Middle-aged women smile at me kindly with horsey yellow teeth. I am happy to abide in the chaos that is not yet the beginning of fruition, knowing that all the while, fruition is here. The walkers are walking fast, heavily held to the earth. Beauty has no time for us. She burns us up and passes on. Something pretty goes on being born in the hearts of the walkers. A strange garland, strung in both directions, they keep coming and going. They never stop.

I read Ecclesiastes in the kitchen. Joy returns in slumps, never explaining its absence. We let it slide.

"I am watching the last of that grasping, striving activity of the mind die," Zero says.

My zeal for manifesting keeps me toiling in this realm. Zero's reluctance to manifest leads him into a realm beyond, where I cannot follow as long as I hold on to the market-place.

He brings mugwort and saint wood. I resign myself to the quietness of the truth.

In me there is the emptiness left after a clamor has ceased. Without an argument, youth has capitulated, leaving behind a woman. Finally, I accept everything.

"Time has passed," I say. "I'm not the same."

"Then you haven't reached yourself yet, because you are beyond time."

In my dream, Tula is a little girl. I give her all my ponies. Carefully I pair them together, the twins, the ones with wings, the old yellow doctor. But she isn't interested.

In the depths of my intention, I see everyone shining, their drops of enlightenment illuminated like dew in the morning sun. I would hesitate to take away the suffering of the beings—they need it so badly.

"It can feel," I think, heartbroken.

Everything that feels is the same thing. The closest thing that feels is the self. I can feel it feeling.

"If you don't get your dreams in this life, they weren't meant to be. You will get them later. Or maybe you will never get them. But even if you are miserable, you can truly enjoy your misery."

I have such a blue feeling. Blue shadows are crawling back in the yellow sun. Fear burns all around me. The birds and animals are discussing it. Naturally, their poetry is different.

The flowers and leaves do not feel thwarted when the conditions are not right for them to exist. Infinite potential is always there.

"What people don't realize is that if they get what they want, it might destroy them," Zero says.

"I see myself when I was on a raft out at sea, with nothing but a little sheet for a sail. I survived that too. I came out at the market place. It was all golden."

A street I have often loved and long. The man sits on the curb, one shin clasped in his brown fingers, the other leg outstretched and lolling on the pavement. A pair of youths squat in cynicism and beer-buzzed joy. The plebeians walk by, tangled into coarse brambles of despair. I recall an unanswered longing.

"The reason the tourists come and consume everything is because they think there is something to be gotten. Where is this thing, they want to know, this thing that is New Orleans? They paid for their ticket and now they are here, hungry for the thing that they've heard about, but they can't see it. They can't see it because they're ignoring everything around them. Then they think there's something wrong with them, something wrong with their life, because they can't find it, because they think other people have found it. Life is not some other thing. It's just life. Life is living."

Pinpoint lights on the porch of the old house fall into the bayou reflecting: magical golden coins. They spread apart and collapse into themselves, sometimes leaving one tiny star behind, swimming in the dark water. I am waiting for the one star to separate again.

It was our season's penance
to finally understand
to take our broken promises
and lead them by the hand

straight on to November
through the shadows of our dreams
to forsake our gilded cages
and come open at the seams

to let our crippled ponies
tarry in the rippling fields
to linger near the end of days
and play at being real

let the poems be our faces
let their lines grow deep and long
let the surface of Lake Pontchartrain
break into a song

could you teach me to be poor in spirit
on the river shore
could you bear this weight of captive freight
safely to its source

could you shatter my mythology
and pull my statues down
lay the generals of granite
among the lilies on the ground

crush them into medicine
to cure us of our doubts
their crystal fears look like tears
while they're running out

13

The cities of the empire, tall-built, honoring something already forgotten. The mind erects impenetrable citadels. The mind assembles impossible gauntlets. The mind poisons experience with tinctures of failure, with plagues of rejection. But the God-mind heals the thoughts, coats and penetrates them with heat, with weal, quiets them with the deep quiet of certainty, with the deepest and most tending kind of awe.

All things flow from a deep well of resting and renewal. All things are finished there. Nostalgia is the smell of that place. It is the place where self-love is perfect, where works are completed, and there is nothing left to be done.

This is the truth: I am a handful of ash. A nest of winds is the home of the ego mind, the mind that calculates. Even language must go. This self who contemplates death will not be here the next time I look. The things done, the photos taken, the piles of moments—where will the care be found with which to steward them?

It is not accurate to say, "I am ready to be dust." It is the dust that speaks. It is the dust that recognizes itself. The words themselves are dust, dust of history, playing in the wind, not anxious about the wind, but in friendship with the wind.

"Only those without a name are at home in this world," Merton wrote.

I travel on this melancholy. This pain is my road. The sadness, the hollowness, is engine, is fire, is fuel. The emptiness stretches out the stuff-ness, as the road stretches the journey.

Love anoints the body, a libation, furrows of regret in its wake.

Zero, with balm in his eyes.

I come to the underpass and hear the song of traveling without getting anywhere.

Zero speaks again of hollows.

"I'm a lonely person," he says, "and I don't care much about being alive. I know that I could die tomorrow and it wouldn't matter, because I would just be dead. I told you about the time I was with the dust. It was a real breakdown; I broke down every barrier that was in my mind. I love that place, but there's no room here for that. People don't have a place for so much stillness."

A music machine in my dream: outside a music was to begin that would never end. Each person would be alone in her own music, forever.

Most of the stories are lost. They were lost in the burning wind of love. But stories keep being born. We cannot remember them all.

I wrote as if I was coining money. I piled up riches of words, each word a coin, a great sum I compiled—as if to buy my freedom. But no one could give me freedom, no matter what price I might pay: I had been free all along.

People under the bridge in stages of repose. One man is shaking out his blanket—the sun's fingers through the columns of cement.

The sky takes heavy breaths.

James begins to sing the Ave Maria. A tall, bearded man pauses to listen, resting his beer can on a defunct newspaper box. A woman with big fake breasts smiles over her shoulder. A woman with a face of wrinkles passes me, her eyes downcast, carrying many things. A man and a woman pull their cameras from their pockets. A homeless man sits down on a crate and removes a shoe. The flamingos on the balcony whirl in the wind. A man with gold teeth talks to himself in an angry voice.

The sun is softened by a thick layer of cloud—it is gentle on the faces of people walking in the street. Some seem happy, their souls pure and blameless in the breeze. My heart wrestles. A very small man strolls by, hand in hand with a woman in a baby-doll dress, tattoos sprawled across her chest. Enlightenment remains, regardless of the circumstances. It does not wait, not even for a moment, for things to be different.

Clouds are sliding down the hill of the sky. Quickly they are sliding, white clouds in blue sky. I cannot find a word for them. A painted man in a top-hat poses for a photo, the inside of his cape shining green. A sad and lonely man sits on top of the garbage can, watching the street. Now and then the sun is swept free and casts shadows everywhere, kisses things with pearls of light. Enlightenment: on both sides of death. Everything you do plants seeds of enlightenment in others.

Listening to the heavy rush of the highway. People are pressing hard, getting to work. On the concrete of Basin Street, I say, "I'm in heaven." This is paradise. Tour guides against the white wall of St. Louis Cemetery. Double-decker buses, empty, skirt the French Quarter. I feel so many humans waking up in dismay.

Sitting on the brink of the abyss, lanterns for eyes. The crackle of thought, colors shooting from the mind. Long arms of self-protection flow from the basic ignorance, the wrong belief. I cannot find the ignorance, I only see its long boughs—schemes, impulses. I do this so that that may be possible, so that the other thing comes to pass— and eventually I will be free, left alone with my fruition. I forget the fruit at hand, the one I am embodying. I am the one perched on the edge of the abyss, watching the strange colors in the fire. Now and then someone tosses in another relic of civilization. I watch it explode, green and white.

I feel spirits swirling around me and through me. And I am a spirit, in possession of a body. I give my sickness to an angel, a little mound of dirt in the angel's hands. He takes it down to where it is needed and it disperses in a glittering cloud. I am different now. I am not the same as I was before.

The sun goes on shining on your wrinkles as it shone on your baby cheeks: it is still today.

We were always in the flower. We are the flower, roaming around in itself.

A man walks into the street. He is wearing a kilt. I have

seen him before, everything he owns hanging from his bicycle. He puts a dollar into the accordionist's hand. He crosses the street, his eyes on the sky, and asks me for a poem to the South wind.

"Life is suffering," Buddha said, "but there is a way out." But life is suffering and a way out. Suffering and the way out are locked in an essential embrace.

I feel as if I had never before opened my eyes. The kindness of being, the wellness that gathers around me. It is given that I am a living person. It's absurd, but I accept it. Consciousness accepts it, like the absurdities of a dream. My eyes drink in the attic window, brilliant in a deep lilac sky.

The world is still high-ceilinged above me. Still full of wonder and possibility. Zero is here, in the grass, talking about his guitar string. His face is wrinkled in the sunlight, bearing heavy weights. Every shadow he can find, he picks it up, he sews it into his clothes, he holds it to his face like a bouquet of flowers.

His great-grandfather was Irish, and his great-grandmother Cherokee. On his mother's side, "gypsies," he says, escaped slaves from Mississippi.

Merton writes of the way he looks, scarred by hell-fires. When he met Henry Miller, they acknowledged their mutual ugliness: "We all exist, thank God."

Zero: "Everyone wants to believe that they have a future. That they aren't going to die soon, and that their future holds some possibility of them achieving their ultimate happiness. But I want to become sages. I want to know that I have no future, and the Devil may care."

The darkness comes and hollows out the rounded fruits. The vast water asks me again, "What do you mean?" A pelican folded up, perched on a post. The gulls, simple, thinking not of other paths, at one with the grey evening. Nothingness of the trees, the water. The water pushes against the concrete steps. This is the cut of things. This is water, this is the wall. See them interact, forever splashing, rocking. It's elegant and bored. I am grateful for the hollow sadness, carving me a new ground.

Samantha tells me her symptoms, the demon she has carried. "My first memory is wishing I would die," she says. "I prayed about it. So I could go to heaven."

An uneasy feeling, as before a coming storm. Elections are coming, people speak of them grimly. There is no hope of a good outcome.

Lonely like a tiger, growing dangerous. Piles of guilt and shame. Neuroses splintering, madness and grief.

"It's storming," I say.

I am deep, beyond words, refracted. Depressed, like a mirror bent into a bowl, reflecting its own darkness. I claw at something enormous.

My skin is a coat of open doors. The world walks in and out unhindered. The winter air is full of riddles. Spiderweb clouds in the broom-teeth of the wind. The tangled elegance here. There is no room for doubt, but doubt arrives. She brings no bundles with her—she says she will sleep on the floor. She takes up no room at all.

I'm thinking of strangers in strange lands. The strangeness of the land itself, cold, knife-like. The rocks are written in a language we don't understand. The skies are so thin we could bleed through our skin, spill into the dark, cruel distance. Twin rivers, one for life and one for death. They flow to the sea and return by invisible routes. When they sing they also pray. The people clap and cheer. They know not what they do.

They gleefully devour a promise kept. Each fiend receives his heart's desire, and there's only pillage left. The circus, the cacophony, the love faltering between us, helpless ones upon the earth. A man and a woman in the street, their age unwieldy, like a blanket over them. The homeless man has a rice bag full of blankets, and a girl's furry hat is on his head. He cleans his long fingernails. He stands facing the musicians. He watches and waits. Time has carried off a dream, lured her to the river, hustled her onto a boat. The portrait artist, serene, toothless, quickly sketching his subject. The smoke rising everywhere like angels.

Seems everybody's down on luck. Peter: I've only made $140 this year.

The cold wind whistles through the trees. The wind chimes are wild, the house hums and creaks. I open the oven. Childish dreams fall off like an old skin, and I find myself startled by my nakedness. Whose life am I living? I am not this personality, this cerebral center. I am a breath of living spirit. What then shall I do for this body, this relic of prehistory? Such clawed thoughts fly through these flapping shutters, crowing of goals. She produces documents. She appears in their bureaucracy. Her life sprawls out, self-important, American, wasteful. Enormous dreams wilt and sour. It would be more beautiful if she would hollow out and blow away with the relentless wind. I cling to my solitude, she says.

"We won't even have arms," I say.

"We better use them while we do," Zero says.

"We're all cowards," he says later. "We're all such despicable creatures."

We do not save our world, when we know that we can.

This language, so exquisitely carved into my mind, is the language of killers and pavers of roads.

The smell of Kentucky grass and clover, the great wind pouring over the hills. Where did I come from? What was I doing there? Our pantries and freezers full of the fruits of a land that was dying. Dying in the white man's hands, for shame, dying the death of the wild in the teeth of the stupid machine.

Looking into Zero's eyes, the cold, the heavy limbs of winter outside. The world is dying all around us. The cloudy light is sharp on the gravel of his face. He is blissfully lifting to his lips his own cup of blood.

Why do you go down that road?

He is already far away. In heaven.

Look for the way in which you can best give, not the way in which you can best receive. Blooming, the panicked heart sustained by great energies, unfurling now, its petals slipping over one another in plain sight of the world.

The story is longer than I supposed. Things happen in their own time, in divine time. We talk of death, of our memory disappearing from the world.

"It's beautiful," Zero says, "to return to the mystery. The face of the ocean, the wind."

Incarnation like a cascade, a gushing descent upon the rocks.

Zero tells a story: he saw her from the sky and wanted to be born in a perfect form to love her completely. He fell and shattered on the ground beside her. She cooed and blew away all his wounds. He broke her apart and sent her into eternity. When he wanted to join her, she told him to jump into the arms he couldn't see. He went to the top of the highest mountain and jumped into her invisible arms. His body broke and became food for small creatures and it became the seeds of change for the world.

Rivers of tears poured from both of our masks, down our necks, our chests, to our waists. Just a moment ago the stage was all that was important. Now stages seem futile, so much sawdust in the teeth of a tide. It is with myself that I will have to make peace—not with the public. The one eye of the public overlaps my only eye. The public's third eye, the eye of my storm, the whirlwind wherein my life must disappear. These are the walls of your wave, crashing. These objects fall at the rate of your fall. You fall together, through the floor of this world, into another.

Have you forgotten to look? A flock of birds drags across the sky like a fishing net, or like the turning of a page.

My heart is heavy with secrets and with common knowledge. I am startled by the raindrops falling around me, like someone whose body startles them in their sleep.

The world has patiently given me all I have asked. It is only at the end of this road that I realized I've asked for the wrong things. I am a dimple in God's giant hand, and in me rolls around a glinting gem.

The world is changing and changing is the world. I have deepened and parts of me have disappeared. The grass and the soil are alive with insects, growth, and change. An airplane engine in the sky. A terrible lonesomeness, a question that has no answer.

In my dream, a candle burning was the crucifixion. Sorriness and fear—watchfulness and wariness. The world is in deep thought and may bring forth a shock. It is still and is keeping its heart with the overlooked, the small, the simple things. My love is still here, but her doors have grown vines.

Peddling the heart of the mountain. "We do what we have to do"—there is no greater myth than that. There isn't much we have to do.

Royal Street, askew, its wounds festering, its rancid pools, its latent perversities. Tourists comb the streets in crestfallen cohorts, pigeons play with their shadows. On the balcony over Rouse's Market, small potted trees are in bloom.

Then, things change. The band begins to play. Berenice puts something back in me. A Caribbean rhythm. Words, drums, trombone, applause. Berenice leans back and becomes wind. The heart has been lonely. The keys yellowed, the letter 'a' sticks. Yet there is something old and mellow, made of dreams, that lifts all else like dust on its currents.

"I'll Fly Away," they play in the sunlight, glinting off the trombone. A man pours out the beers and other drinks from the trash can and carries off the cans in a white plastic trash bag. The spilled liquids pool around me in the street. Clouds are couched at the end of the long corridor of the street, the bell tolls. A man in a silver cowboy hat collects tips in a paint bucket. Things have come and gone and come again. Old things are here, the brick chimneys reiterating, the dizzy, waterlogged city, the puzzle of people.

The morning is warm, with a warmth in its golden color. Dreams of blue-green water and poems too blue and green to be heard. I am the last thing the people want to see: their mortality. Heart full of static. Foul smells, urine and cigarette smoke, beers turning sour in the trash.

Many planes converging: this is where it hurts, where people are loving, and where I am not loving enough in return.

This moment blends into other moments. Peter kneels beside me, his tin can of water and a painting sheathed in cardboard under his arm.

"Everything is a lesson," he says.

A man sits on the barricade with a bright blue bucket between his knees, strings of beads around his neck, his head bowed so his face cannot be seen. After the song has ended, the listening crowd walks away. What is left? A few dollars, perhaps. The emptiness on the other side of magic.

I asked the word
what she had to say
but she just winked
and said it's been a long day

I asked the deed
what she meant to do
but she just breathed
and let the moment pass through

and I asked the soul
what she meant to be
but it was so late
it had gotten early

and the soul and the deed
and the word were gone
but the dreamless body
of the world lived on

14

The ghosts are prowling the echoing corridor. An old woman mumbles to herself as she feels her way home in the dark. The sky is scarred and illuminated with the debris of some lost childhood. The musicians have packed away their instruments and the gas-lamps have fluttered awake. The hunger in the pit of my stomach becomes delirium. The lights begin to come from the inside out, instead of the other way around.

I am no longer alone in the wind of dollars. I am together with the ghouls and lost souls, clamoring for recognition and camaraderie. They paw my pockets with their fingers. They pull at my collar and push in my chair. They call forth whatever treasures are left lingering in my spirit and parcel them out amongst themselves. They lift a dark glass to my lips.

The old woman at the end of the bar is weeping, talking to no one about her long-lost love. She met him on these shores fifty years before. They were to be married. Now she has returned, she seems to see him everywhere.

The master of this place: a tall, sallow man. These souls are his bounty and he will deliver them fast into the green hands of morning. As for me, I am broke and so I am free a while longer. I can spill from the swinging door like an old bouquet of flowers for the tourists to trample.

In the fierce winter night, the silence startles me. The planet seems to have never been discovered. The relics of life look pale and strange, unfamiliar as a corpse, dumb objects. I weep for the wavering shadows of the drunks I once knew, it seems only in a dream.

The sky was dark with thunder. In the land of wild beasts in my dream, I had to lie down and accept that I could be eaten by the panther.

War flickers around the edges of things. They have once again drowned our future: an infant in a bathtub. Such a trivial amount of water can end a life when it is small. We do not mourn it, or even speak of it. We never knew it was alive, so how can it be missed?

The skyscrapers lean into darkness, the grottoes and folds of history's emptying. There is so little time left. Yet there is a sweet advent within me. My old age embarrassing, like a pair of dirty underwear I am carrying around in my bag.

The fear and sadness are always here, but I can live with them now as friends. My love is cooking. A calm, wise face. The soft, sad, space around things. My faltering steps into empty fields. Losses fall upon us like an unwanted snow. We wait, knowing worse will come.

The sound of chopping. Engines and the hungry streets. The cynical whistling of a siren. Powerlessness creeping into my hands like disease. A shadow that unites with other shadows to become the night. Questions I put to bed, knowing they shall not wake again.

The rain and lightning. The corn pollinating. I sit back. I am far away. I fall through many frames. I am my voice's voice.

If you look at a flower too long, it withers, she said.

The light moves—it doesn't stay still. That is because it is alive, and life is fleeting. The morning is quiet. Ferns spring up from the wet soil: memories of prehistory. The planets dance. A family of clover, the crawling crabgrass. Mosquitoes in the shadows, fleeing the strong fingers of the sun. Aspire to be like the Buddha, and you may just become a good person.

The train crying. My fingers cold after washing the dishes. The baby bellowing next door. The light pouring out of the lamp. My shame pouring down like rain. The wastes of time. Things are different from how they were before. When we pick up the old books, we can see how much they didn't know. The earth has grown poorer—so much has disappeared forever. Where proud nations once lived there are now cities like mine.

Reality breaks open and slides over itself. A wall of black tiles glitters radically with lights. Two men in long flowing white robes sit in the open back hatch of an SUV, their eyes glazed, smiling, curls of smoke circling their faces. Nearby, the Chinese grocery spills over with luminous forms. A woman's body gleams in the golden, threaded glow.

Suddenly, the wound closes. The lights murmur to themselves, chanting their prayer for freedom, locked eternally in their mechanical pulsing.

Why are you making so much noise? I asked the trees.

They were throwing their old, dry leaves hard upon the crackling carpet of leaves beneath them. Knowing they were beautiful, the yellow blossoms from the vine had fallen softly, without a sound. The vine had withered, but it left its bare ropes around the fence like an unfinished work. Every now and then another flower was sacrificed, too old and imperfect to remain on the bough. A fly walked among the yellow flowers, kissing them with love in spite of their bedraggled state.

Police sirens whistled flirtatiously. The city seemed to blush as the street lamps came on.

I offer my body as food for all beings, that they may eat and be satisfied. I am clothed in wild landscapes, in broad and chalice-shaped trees, strong of arm. The place rejects me, pushes me out of it, cuts me out, and the seams of the world, where I had been, cry out and bleed.

And like that the days are consumed by work. My heart is lighter. I am no longer sad for things that have receded. There are other things here. There are cities within cities. Relatedness to the students. I approach something I know but have forgotten.

This body just a suitcase. Could you make the world smooth by pressing it against your page?

Wind in the trees, leaves falling. All is well, once more. The roar of the highway, a siren chanting. I'm still not me. Yet I am someone.

I feel the axis swaying under me. Certain things are

settled. But there is that momentum within me that disrupts this tranquil, logical flow. That force also exists, and can carry things with it.

The pitter-patter of thoughts, each one on a short leash.

The fearsome darkness out of which we crawled, which split our hands into five fingers. It is no wonder we suffer anxieties, having been forged from the terror of the wild. The glittering dreams give way to gritty realities. My discipline is not nearly enough. It has always been this way.

It feels just like old times, a trumpet on the air, drums in the low currents of the wind, and my heart with nowhere to go.

Under my own spell, hypnotized by the silver tongues in my mind, counseling me, prodding me. How ridiculous they are—a wall of glittering glass, a business front for the hollow shop of death, on the wild highway that will only be here for a while.

I am listening at the mound of the earth, my ear to its heaving heart.

When cessation comes, I find ego beneath the mask of righteous activity. Hide and seek again! Things are easier when the intention is pure: the alleviation of suffering. This aim is not a hard one to achieve. There are as many ways to reach this shore as there are waters that flow to the sea.

The spillway was rushing with water. It looked like an ocean. We saw a lone tree in the midst of a wide plain of marsh grasses, a large bird's nest in its bare arms.

The interior of the church was cool and without windows. The walls were sculpted neatly into the ceiling, perfectly white. Knicknacks—a nativity scene—were arranged on shelves. In the chapel, each seat was covered in dark blue velvet.

The preacher thanked the Lord that we had been awakened and given a mission and the wherewithal to achieve it. He said that our mission was that the children would grow up and live healthy lives, and not be poisoned, and that all kinds of diseases and infirmities not befall the people of the community as they have been. He prayed that the governor would feel something stirring and troubling his mind, and that there should be a stirring and a moving in the valley of death, a rattling of the bones. He prayed that we might be like Moses and say, "Let my people go." He prayed that we might be flanked by angels to both sides, before us, and to the rear.

I stood outside with two elder women who were speaking with frustration about the lack of support and involvement from the larger community. They turned their attention to the weather and one said, gazing at a pair of trees growing on the other side of the driveway, "I bet these trees have secrets. I bet they talk about a lot of stuff."

Before the cameras, the older preacher in the blue suit says, "There's no rights a black man has that a white man is bound to respect. So it said in the Dred Scott decision. Then, there was a civil war, and at the end of it, our ancestors became free and they bought this land, and this was theirs. Then, they began to put petrochemical plants here, creating

249

diseases too numerous to mention."

The clouds can talk, but forget their lines.

"Money is my mother and my father." This flashing coin falls into the dark waters of my mind.

For whom am I performing? All has come to nothing. There is only one mirror, there is no mirror. Spiritual rain. All was always destined for nothing, for what then do I mourn?

Something in my dreams: the way their mystery worked, a veil of magic they lived behind. The symmetry and simplicity of the one who didn't carry many words, but spoke in stones and feathers and mandalas. He walked with the light—I never saw him stray. Even in his shadow he was prayerful, repentant. Was he the rock upon which their castle was built?

There were others—the visionary, the friend, the scientist. They were so perfectly the kaleidoscope of the self. We could open a door or a window, turn a corner, and look upon them. And we did, and we wondered. We always thought there would be more.

Let go of being trapped on the other side of magic, of being kept from that golden glow. The self is only crying out because the roots of her action must be tended—it is not about her but about her relatedness to the ground-web that nourishes the community.

Noticing the way each person reflects off the others. Each one has a particular shine, an incredible gift. I can see the way they all fit together, the light they shed on one another, and I can see my place among them—I can see how they see and feel me, the gravity of myself as it pulls on them.

It is strange to look at oneself from the outside. My own gentleness, this soft, prodding murmur upon which my thoughts and actions seem to ride. So earnest and insistent. Its synthetic, manufactured quality—an echo of many generations of female voices cooing to their daughters, yet hypnotized by its own lullabye, not aware of itself as a contrivance. It's like seeing a ghost walking around in your house, not knowing that she is dead. We just float around, lost in ourselves, mesmerized by reflections of our predicament wherever we can find them.

The truth doesn't have time for us. Her flowers are carnivorous; their mouths are red with our blood. Her swollen clouds bear our tears away where we cannot see them. Her glorious new seasons leave us evacuated, reduced to rubble.

But the pink new winds of morning bring my love's hair into my hands. The sky is a moving map, swirling with ancestors. The banana trees know me and have taught me the right way. My heart is a woman on the roadside, carrying everything she owns on her back. She can't unwrap her burden until she gets to where she's going. Almost she has forgotten what she carries.

Thankful I am for the oceans within me, and thankful I am for the oceans without. My coiled up rivers and the river with no mouth. The heavy waters that carry the weightless light.

In these children, the past unfurls once more. I cannot push this river to the right or the left with my bare hands. Some big heavy money will have to do it, and by then it will be too late.

Place me then in the smirk of the exiled world. In her shady dimple let me rest and look on. Now and then when some big man comes along, let me stick out my foot and make him fall. It won't be the last laugh, but after so many tears, it's unavoidable.

My mind is plagued and troubled. I do not know the past or future. A kite rocks to and fro, tethered by an invisible line. The clouds apologize and cover our faces. A ghostly voice echoes in the stopped streetcar that simply waits, as if for the end.

I'm sorry, the bayou says, and marches single-file to the stadium. The oak branches sift the air, undecided. My heart has taken a long and winding, silent and solitary way, and only now remembers it had forgotten where it was going.

Here and there, chimes weigh in on the matter. A bell tolls. There is much space between sounds, much time between moments. Things are hidden there. I am not so alone. The men fall back, leaving the women with their glowing windows in the dusk. The streetcar has moved on, but another has taken its place.

It takes so much to believe. Such a heavy weight must be lifted. At the same time, I sustain the world effortlessly.

The parade of cars going home. The trees whisper. They know it is so. The tires scream against the road. Everything points toward the heart; everything shatters the heart as if made for that purpose.

I believe you. I return. The bayou clasps the light of a stolen fire. I can give up the complicated sums of life and death. Life and death are only the debris that floats to me on the wind. They come and go, like balled-up receipts. My heart is on a trackless path through dark waters.

Lavender Ink
New Orleans
lavenderink.org

Made in the USA
Middletown, DE
05 August 2020